THREE GENERATIONS
of LOVE

JAMES POPE

Archway Publishing books may be ordered through booksellers or by contacting:

Archway Publishing
1663 Liberty Drive
Bloomington, IN 47403
www.archwaypublishing.com
844-669-3957

ISBN: 978-1-6657-5183-4 (sc)
ISBN: 978-1-6657-5184-1 (e)

Library of Congress Control Number: 2023919744

Print information available on the last page.

Archway Publishing rev. date: 10/17/2023

MOVING FORWARD

THREE GENERATIONS OF LOVE (aka 3GL), the second of my three uniquely connected novels. On the back cover is the story line. Also, "UREKA", a 360-page screenplay from the novel, using the same name.

My first novel POST HOLE DIGGER is the story of my life from first memory to age 19, also a screenplay. My third novel STEPPING STONES to the ARCH PLEASURE is my life of intimacy, also a screenplay.

If you have questions/feedback for me, go to my website www.pope-jim.com for communication.

James Pope

CHAPTER ONE

The rolling verdant expanse of the Ironwood Golf Course stretched away, emerald and vivid under the cloudless Nebraska summer sky. The fairways meandered through a mature longleaf pine forest and around pristine lakes. The chatter of a women's foursome, interspersed with laughs and giggles, echoed in the morning stillness. Julia March set up on the third hole for a tee off shot, her shapely, lean, tanned legs and short shorts making the stunning brunette look taller than her five feet five. Her blonde, blue-eyed partner Beth Sampson's gaze lasered into Julia as she made her swing, which was in good form with a picturesque follow-through. Julia muttered, "Damn, I was off-balance. The shot went wild and into the trees." The two attractive women coming up behind them were part of their foursome, and a lot of good-natured kidding followed Julia as she headed toward the trees.

Beth called "I'll help you find the ball" and followed her.

One of the other women said, "We'll play on through. I have a feeling that is going to be a hard-to-find ball."

The other woman turned to her friend. "Beth is getting to be like a bitch in heat with Julia. I think they have to get on the same path."

"Amen, sister, amen."

Fifteen minutes later, when Julia and Beth caught up with them at the fourth hole, Julia looked flushed. As she buttoned the top button of her golf shirt, one of the others called, "My, that ball must have been lost in the deepest part of the woods. Hope you found it with no trouble." Someone giggled.

Beth stuck out her tongue at them. "Don't be catty, girls."

They played on through the whole eighteen-hole course. Later after the match, Julia and Beth found themselves alone in the shower. Beth, leering, watched Julia emerging from the shower stall and approached her. The brunette stood back, wrapping a towel around herself, saying, "Knock it off, Beth. This is one of the most exclusive clubs in town. You'll get us kicked out. I couldn't afford a scandal like that. My husband's company would probably let him go in a minute if we got caught."

Beth pouted. "Nobody's in here but us. As I remember, you used to be more adventuresome."

Julia said nothing and started to work on her hair.

Beth was miffed now. "Damn it, Julia, I'm getting tired of fighting for a piece of you. When are you going to do something about your life?"

Julia turbaned a towel around her wet hair and intoned, "My life is just fine, thank you. David is doing great in the oil business, and I'm lucky to have him after the romantic luck I've had—a two-faced son of a bitch who left me high and dry and with a kid to bring up by myself. So I consider myself damn lucky, and you should too. Nothing interferes with our little rendezvous. Don't jinx me for my luck."

"Yeah, luck with men. I keep telling you there's no such thing as a bisexual. You wouldn't enjoy women so much if there was. You're either one or the other, and I don't care what the shrinks say. You just want a husband for someone to take care of you."

Julia was drying her hair now and said, "What's wrong with that? I have a daughter to raise and no real work skills. All I have is me, and babe, I have to make it work for me." Both were quiet while Julia got dressed. "Besides, Beth, the locker room isn't the place to discuss this. Please put it aside for now. You know the walls, especially around here, have ears. And the girls are waiting for us in the lounge. Remember, we have that golf tournament to plan."

Beth was still petulant. "Golf tournament, shmolf tournament."

Julia was enjoying her second martini and nibbling on some delicious-looking hors d'oeuvres. Frannie, one of their foursome, gazing around, murmured below her breath, "Look at all these middle-aged ladies making believe that they are here for any other reason than trolling for men."

Beth interjected, "Yeah, they all love golf so much." "Yeah, as much as Tiger Woods," someone said.

This provoked a smatter of smirks and cynical giggling. Although some of these women were bisexual, almost all preferred women.

Julia's cell phone chirped and played the theme from Rocky. Before she picked it up, one of the girls commented, "Why did you pick such a macho theme song, Julia?"

Beth cracked, "She thinks it's good cover."

Julia raised her brows and answered the phone. She listened for a moment and then said, "Hey, Mom."

On the other end of the line Julia's mom, Hazel, an attractive older woman, well proportioned and fit, said in a whining tone, "I still haven't heard back from you about the fishing trip."

Julia didn't hide the roll of her eyes. "Isn't that still months away?"

"Julia, your father doesn't ask much of you. So we go on a fishing trip once a year."

"Okay, okay. Look, I can't talk about it right now. I'm with the girls at the golf club." She listened again. "Okay, okay, how about… Thursday at six? I'll throw something together for dinner, and we'll plan the trip, okay?"

"Okeydokey. We'll be there."

There was a pause on the line, and although Julia was eager to be done with the call, she asked, "Mom? You there?"

Frannie leaned over to Beth and asked, "Is Mom getting a little hard of hearing?"

"Hell, no. Have you ever seen her mom?" Frannie shook her head.

"Drop-dead gorgeous. For any age. I wouldn't mind doing her myself."

Julia heard her mother say, "Okay, dear. Hey, will you send David over as soon as you can? I have an electrical problem here."

"Can't it wait?"

"You want the house to burn down?"

That was Hazel, always the drama queen. Julia had grown up with it and knew better than to argue with her. "Okay, Mom, I'll ask him to stop by."

Julia turned to Beth with a righteous smirk. "See what I mean? I'll ask David to go over and check out her problem, and he'll gladly do it. What other husband would go out of his way to fix things for his mother-in-law. Don't tell me that he isn't a great catch. And a great stepdad for Ashley." Beth didn't answer but simply took another sip of her martini.

The girls got so carried away with the martini-heavy lunch and female chatter they didn't make much progress on the plans for the tournament, so Julia suggested they carry on at her house.

Julia and Beth were riding together, and they pulled up at the sprawling ranch- style home surrounded with hundred-year-old trees and in deep shade of the treeless Nebraska plains. But for Omaha, this was a unique feature of the upscale neighborhood of Ralston.

Talking about their kids, Julia mentioned Ashley had only one thing on her mind. Beth raised a brow. "Men?"

"You got it. I'm lucky she's not knocked up yet. A couple of girls in her dorm are already sporting baby bumps. Sheesh! You'd think it was a badge of honor. These kids today, they've got those damn iPhones and they send pictures of themselves all over the net, bare ass, getting the boys all hot and bothered. Did you know that some of the kids—even high school kids—are into threesomes? And all that here in conservative old Nebraska. You could see it in the big cities on the coasts, but here in Nebraska?"

As the ladies settled in the living room, Julia went upstairs and popped into Ashley's room. The teenager was stretched across the bed, on her belly, one foot swinging, her thumbs furiously working her smartphone. Julia hesitated a moment before launching into her tirade. Ashley—at five four, with auburn hair—had a figure far too voluptuous for a teen. She was wearing a T-shirt, no panties. Her bare butt curved up from her back in the most amazing way, giving her the appearance of a marble statue sculpted to perfection.

Her mouth forming an O, Julia whined, "For cripes' sakes, Ashley, put something on. Lying there with your butt up in the air."

"For God's sakes, Mom, you're the only one here in the afternoon. What's the big deal?"

"Well, my golf girls are all downstairs. I don't want you wandering around the house like that. It's... it's just unseemly, young lady. Put something on," she fired at her. "And do you spend your whole life texting? God forbid you ever lose your thumbs, you'd have no life."

Ashley, feigning exasperation, whined, "Sheesh, Mom, who loses their thumbs?"

"Anyway—"

"And if I did, texting would be the least of my worries."

"Look, then do something useful and text David and tell him that my parents are coming for dinner Thursday about the goddamned fishing trip. And, oh," she said before leaving, "tell him to stop by Grandma's about an electrical problem she's having."

Ashley said, "Grandma's a hoot. Does she think David has nothing to do but fix her house?" Then she began texting away.

In his office in downtown Omaha, high up in one of the city's newest skyscrapers, David, a farm-boy type with an athlete's body and wholesome good looks, picked up his cell phone. It was Ashley. He typed. "Ashley, I'm trying to work here."

He read, "The GPs are coming over for dinner Thursday (boring). They want to talk about the fishing trip."

David wrote, "Oh yeah, the goddamned fishing trip. How could I forget?"

He read more. "I'm only wearing a T-shirt, no panties! Wish you were here!" David's face turned crimson. And he typed furiously. "Jesus, Ashley! Don't text that! Christ! This stuff goes all over the world. How many times have I told you about stuff like that? Knock it off."

Ashley loved to embarrass David with her flirtatious ways. After she put down her iPod, she went over to her dresser and took out her diary. She also grabbed a pen and threw herself back across the bed and started writing.

Mom gets more distant from David every day. Seeing the dykey of friends she has, that's not a surprise. True, they're not bad looking, but women doing women? Yuck! I can't see their marriage lasting very long now. If he doesn't find out on his own, I'll find some way to let him know. I'm sure a stud like David won't put up with that. Well, I'm a college woman now and enough woman to fill that void in David's life. Even right now, I'm more of a woman for him than Mom.

She glanced over at a picture on her dresser. It was of a wedding party. And she was the adorable little flower girl. Who could have known that the little girl standing next to David at their wedding would one day be his lover? Well, not his girlfriend actually, but she felt in her bones that he liked her. Better than he liked Mom.

Eyeing the wedding picture, she remembered how much she resented, or should she say hated, her mother for taking her real daddy away from her. This new guy, David, wasn't her dad. He was cute, but he wasn't Daddy. But he was so nice to her that in no time at all she had forgotten all about her father. David became her main focus now.

CHAPTER TWO

David pulled up in his car, parked, hopped out, and headed for Hazel's front door. He rang the bell and waited.

Hazel called out, "It's open."

And David let himself in. "It's me!"

Approaching him while belting her bathrobe, she grinned. The grin evolved into a wide smile, "Coming! Well, not yet…"

David, veiling a smirk but a bit exasperated, said, "You can't just say 'It's open,' Hazel. Might be a damned serial killer."

"No, it's just you," she said. "Serial killer, I doubt it. Serial satyr, maybe." "Come on, Hazel, a satyr is someone who can't get enough sex. You're enough woman for any man."

While his gaze fixed on her, she turned her back to him and lowered her robe. The robe slipped down over a lean back flaring out to a womanly butt and slim long legs. With lust, his eyes found their way up and down her body as he absorbed her magnificent form.

David, with his own Cheshire grin, said, "I might be a horndog, but I always get permission."

Hazel walked into his arms and said, "Yeah, nobody ever says no to you, so you don't havta rape anyone."

David, now wearing a wide smile, said, "Another naked lunch. Don't ever change the menu. After all this time the will-you game still works."

"I don't see it ever changing," she said as she took him by the hand and headed toward the bedroom.

There was no coyness or embarrassment between the two. Their lovemaking, by now, had taken on a pattern that had not yet succumbed to boredom. They were as excited by each other as if it were the first time. He knew his way around her voluptuous body as well as she knew her way around his. Both were fully aware of what turned the other on and wasted no time getting to it. Their coupling was animated and enthusiastic. Soon, covered with a sheen of sweat, they parted and gasped for breath. Incredulous, he said, "Are you sure that you're older than me?"

She smiled. "Maybe I just have more vigor for it than you. After all, my best days are behind me."

He turned to her and said, "Only one of your assets is behind you. The rest is all up front." He cupped one full breast and mouthed the nipple. "I doubt that your best days are behind you. I truly do."

Later, as usual they dozed off, but David's mind was not ready to shut down yet. As Hazel slept, something—maybe it was déjà vu of some kind—drew him back to his youth. He was again back at Avoca High School, about forty miles from Omaha.

He was seventeen again, and it was twenty-one years ago. Avoca High was the breeding ground for many a future relationship. Young hearts stirred every day. Many could not settle on one or another person. Teenage intrigue abounded. Of course, the main criterion still was the ancient first impression. That person who made one's heart flutter, gave him shortness of breath, one whom he feared most talking to. At least until a relationship took hold. And then it was still more about looks than it was about relationships.

When David caught sight of Julia outside of the science lab, he called out, "Julia! Hey, Julia!"

She at first didn't seem to hear him. He called again. Finally she turned. "Yes, David?"

"Are we on for tonight?"

Almost dismissively, she called back "Sure, sure!" and quickly turned back to her girlfriends.

He waved happily, turned on his heel, and was on his way.

That night, Julia was before her mirror in her second-floor bedroom, putting the final touches on her hair. Even though she kept her hair longer and in a ponytail, it still required a lot of work to keep it looking natural and not coiffed. She was still busy when a car horn honked outside. Hurrying to the window, she gave an enthusiastic wave and the one-finger "one second" signal.

As Julia bounded down the stairs, her ponytail bouncing, a younger Hazel, looking out the window at the unfamiliar car, commented, "That doesn't look like David's car."

"It's not. It's Alan's!"

"Thought you were going with David?"

Julia was barely listening as she tugged at her hair in the hallway mirror. Seeing her mother's disapproving eyes in the mirror, behind her, Julia said, "I was going with David but then Alan called."

"What did David say?"

Rolling her eyes in exasperation, Julia declared, "Oh my god, Mom. Who cares what David would say? After all, Alan's family is one of the richest families in town, and his car is so cool. There's nothing, absolutely nothing, binding me to David. I'm not wearing his sweater, his ring—nothing."

"Well, what did David say?"

Julia, her exasperation mounting, said, "I don't know. I didn't tell him. I really didn't have time. Alan called me late. If he calls, you can tell him anything you want. Tell him I had to visit a sick friend."

"Julia! You can't just stand the boy up!"

The teenager simply shrugged and hurried toward the door, muttering, "He'll live."

Hazel grabbed her by the arm and demanded, "You call him right now, young lady!"

She whined, "Mom! I don't want to keep Alan waiting. He's the grooviest guy in school."

"I didn't raise you to be so thoughtless about other people's feelings, young lady. You go to that phone and call."

Julia resisted. Then, in order to facilitate her getting out the door, she picked up the phone and called David. It was a short and perfunctory conversation, after which Julia dashed out the door.

David, having resigned himself to an evening shooting pool with his buddies, didn't have his heart into the game at Hart's Pool Room on Main Street. He kept swigging on a Coke and taking an inordinate amount of time chalking his cue.

His buddy Tommy kept complaining, "Hey, come on, man. If we were on the basketball court, they'd have called you for delay of game."

David ignored him, definitely not into his game. "Chill out, Tommy. I'm setting up my shot. Difference between champions like me and hackers like you is lining up the shots."

Just before he was about to pull the trigger on his shot, he spotted a couple walking by the poolroom. He had no trouble recognizing Julia. In a second, he made out Alan Harper too. They seemed happy, beaming and chattering. *Going out with the girls to cheer up a friend, huh? I should have known.* He missed the shot, scratching. Further embarrassment followed when the cue ball hit the floor and began rolling. Other players looked up, grinning at the hapless David.

Tommy was rolling his eyes. "Man, why do you keep chasing that chick?" "What do you mean?"

"You know what I mean. You told me you couldn't shoot pool tonight because you had a date with Julia. I just saw her out on a date, and it wasn't with you."

"Shut up, Tommy!"

"I'm telling you straight, man. The chick's making a fool of you." David furiously chalked his pool cue.

Tommy lit a cigarette. "Know what they're callin' you on the team these days?" David wanted to fake he didn't care, but he did, very much.

At first, he said nothing. Eventually, it got the best of him. "What?" he asked.

"What did they use to call you because you control the ball so well, all that between-the-leg stuff and keeping low to the ground so the ball don't get stolen?"

"Yeah, what about it?"

"Well, what did they call you?" "Fastball March. Why?"

"Know what they call you nowadays?"

David didn't want to hear whatever it was, but he couldn't stand it. "What?" "No-Balls March."

David slammed the pool stick into the rack and stormed off into the night.

He knew Tommy wasn't lying. He had made such a fool of himself swooning over Julia that he was ashamed of himself and vowed to give her up.

Of course, he had made that vow before.

About three weeks later, a picture started circulating around school on smartphones. It was of Alan under some naked girl who was evidently riding him. The girl's face couldn't be seen, but her body looked familiar. Alan's hand was partially covering a tattoo on the rise of her butt. It looked like part of a butterfly, and he knew who had a butterfly on their butt.

He confronted Julia at her house. He knew nobody was home, and he was furious when he stormed in. He asked, "Is this you and Alan?"

She looked at the smartphone and laughed, which infuriated him. "I've seen that. Some joker is circulating it. It's not me, I can tell you that."

He simply glowered at her, his face red. Then she said, "Look, David. What's it to you anyway? You and I aren't pinned or anything. We haven't planned a future. We get out of high school this year, and I don't see you have anything going for you."

"I'm gonna work at Waverly on the work co-op program. Go to UNebraska and then work six weeks."

"That's gonna take a million years. I want to get married while I'm still young." "I suppose Alan is going to marry you right away."

With a bit of a smirk, she said, "Maybe he is."

David left the house in a rage he could hardly control. He wanted to punch something hard. He had never felt so much pain in his life. She was like a drug to him. He wanted her so bad it hurt. And she was so damn cocky and rotten about it. They had dated on and off all through high school. How could she blow him off so easily?

At graduation, he could barely get the words out while, during the excitement of the festivities, he told her, "I hope you get what you want."

She very flippantly said, "Thanks, David."

CHAPTER THREE

David had taken the technical course for his high school curriculum in order to prepare himself for a college engineering degree. He was off-again, on-again with Julia—sure he was becoming second choice to Alan Harper and only getting a date when Harper wasn't available or didn't ask her out.

The memories kept coming back like an old-time movie reel. This morning of his senior year, the class was on a field trip to the Waverly Machine Company, the largest manufacturer of oil-drilling equipment in town. Uncharacteristically, this morning he seemed more interested in the workings of the assembly line than he was with Julia, who tagged along with the rest of the senior girls, completely bored. So when, out of sheer boredom, Julia approached him and struck up a conversation, he was only a bit interested as she was taking his mind off the technical aspects of their trip. When Alan approached and whisked her away, he was only a bit sad and quickly took up his interest where he left off. The mechanics of the Waverly assembly line was the only thing that would get his interest from Julia. This was important and no time for idle chatter with a girl.

Unlike most assembly line workers who found the line the most boring, monotonous kind of work, David was fascinated by it because he was into the intricate mechanisms that made it work. And he kept his eyes on every facet of the operation. Although there were strict rules about women's clothes on the assembly line, every once in a while, someone slipped by with a loose belt or scarf.

One day, during his college work program at Waverly and while acting as supervisor, David heard a scream. A panicked woman at the end of the line was struggling, trying to get her loose belt out of the machinery, but it was dragging her along. David was too far from the off switch, and he could see that disaster for the woman was imminent. He knew that the machinery was dragging her along and the next part of the conveyor belt could do her serious harm. He quickly jammed a wrench into the cog mechanism at just the right point, causing the unit to jam to a stop and short out. He helped the weeping woman extricate her belt from the machinery. Waverly Management saw something special in David and was on his side at the inquest of the accident board that followed. The union charged that it was Waverly Machinery's responsibility for the accident. Although the woman wasn't physically hurt, she suffered trauma and had to be treated.

The policy at Waverly was that in order to keep the production line moving without stop, the supervisory shift changed at odd intervals. This meant that the supervisor who was taking over had to sign the form of the previous supervisor stating all safety precautions had been made. So when David took over, he signed a waiver that he had inspected the crew and everybody clothing-wise was in compliance. Of course, there really was no time for him to inspect the entire assembly line crew. It was more or less a formality.

That was the way it was supposed to work. David was not responsible for checking the clothing and attire of the workers on the shift he was taking over. Yet it would be prudent, time permitting to do so. Yet time was never permitting. David was in the clear but that did not satisfy him.

He testified to the accident board that in order to change shifts safely, the line would have to be shut down so the new supervisor could check the personnel. Now theoretically, they had already been checked, but the following things had happened in the past: A woman got chilly and wrapped a scarf around her neck—a safety hazard since the scarf could get caught in the machinery. Another woman decided to change the belt on her slacks because it was not comfortable, yet the new belt was longer—another safety hazard. A man wearing a long-sleeve shirt decided to let the sleeves down because he was chilly—another safety hazard.

David reported to the union accident board that since the company would lose money by reinspecting the attire on every shift, everyone should wear a standardized, approved one-piece uniform with nothing sticking out to be caught in the machinery.

His idea was not only accepted by the union, but the company also agreed. Something they rarely did with the union.

David was seen as a comer, and his career crept steadily uphill.

They had been noticing David anyway, but this rescue raised him in their estimation. They admired his keen understanding of the machinery and the line operation.

One day he found himself sitting before the line supervisor. "David, I've been hearing and seeing good things about you. You really understand your job and beyond your job."

"Thanks, sir, it's just that the equipment fascinates me and so it's easy for me." "Glad to hear it, David. We usually don't promote people before their junior year at college, but we're going to promote you to line supervisor for the second floor. Does that suit you?"

Beaming, David said, "Yes, sir, it does. Thank you very much."

Upon graduation from high school and unable to afford full-time tuition at the University of Nebraska, he had enrolled in a work-school program that divided his time between six weeks of school and then off to six weeks on the assembly line at Waverly. He was quite happy with the arrangement as it was highly unlikely he would have been able to go to college at all.

David was seeing less and less of Julia, who was seeing more and more of Alan. She was certain that she had the rich boy hooked. They had been having sex regularly, and she was sure that she would soon be his wife. She didn't even like sex with Alan but played the game to gain the prize. She actually enjoyed sex with two girls at school, neither of whom knew of the other. But both were very discreet. Back then, gay relationships were not so liberal. But one morning at work, Julia arrived at her job at Safeco Insurance to find a gaggle of her coworker girlfriends gathered around a newspaper laid out on a desk. When she approached, they dispersed like a bunch of roaches under a bright light. Only one, her particular nemesis, Carol Copeland, stood her ground.

There was a smirk bordering on evil on Jane's face as she said, "Did you see the morning daily news?"

Julia shook her head. It didn't take her long to find Alan's name on the engagements page. He was marrying Carol Copeland, who was not only thirty and beautiful, but her family was also as rich as the Harpers. It was rumored that Carol not only put out, but she was also into everything. Alan's engagement to Carol was announced with all the details. Julia hung her head low and headed for her desk. Getting through the rest of the day without showing her remorse was one of the toughest things she ever did in her life.

By the time most seniors were done with their work-study program at Waverly, they were lucky to still have a job. David had advanced to general foreman, responsible for operations for the whole second shift.

CHAPTER FOUR

After college, David was living the bachelor life, with a nice apartment and a new Jeep. Things were pretty good, except for the lingering heartbreak over Julia.

One day, David was busy in his office when his boss DH entered the room, looking enthusiastic. "Dave, how would you like to spend some time in Hawaii?"

"Hawaii?"

"Right, our Pacific Rim customer service rep has some serious health problems and has to take time off, maybe permanently. You know all our equipment and what it takes to keep it running. I'm recommending you for the job. I always say, if you can't stand the cold, get in the kitchen." He chuckled at his lame joke.

David took no time to think. This would be the opportunity of a lifetime for any young man, let alone one who badly needed a change of scenery and the chance to meet new people. He said, "I'll start packing and put my stuff in storage."

When he was transferred to the Honolulu office, he knew that the change would do him good. And it seemed to. There were so many new sights and places and people that he was soon deep into his new life. The sweeping reaches of the amazingly blue Pacific were enough to set a prairie farm boy's heart fluttering.

The fast-paced rackety rack of the island bands' rhythms, the swaying of grass skirts, the rustle in the palm fronds from an offshore breeze—all seemed to morph him from mainlander to a genuine islander.

Life was moving along in a contented way for him when two letters came in one morning—letters that rocked his world, one more so than the other. The first was from his mother, which he opened with a shiny new letter opener. Out dropped a newspaper clipping. It was Julia's wedding announcement. He stared at it for a while, his jaw loose, his eyes wide. Sure, he had succumbed to the disappointment that he had lost Julia, but this—a wedding announcement. This hurt. First love was the hardest to get over. At the time, Julia had been everything to him. The rest of the information seemed almost superfluous.

His mother wrote, "I don't think that she's known this guy very long. I think she is just marrying the first guy to come along after being dumped by Alan. More depressing news had to do with the family farm. Due to the myriad things that affect farming, her parents, John and Hazel, lost the farm, and both are now working in the city."

It took David quite a while to open the next letter as he was still smarting from the first letter. His pride had never allowed him to call Julia after Alan married someone else. Maybe somewhere in the far corners of his mind, he harbored the idea of trying for her again, but this newspaper announcement ended that. And reading the wedding announcement was like reading about a long-lost friend, almost like an obituary. Too far in the past to mean much to him now, yet it hurt.

So when he got around to opening the second letter, it was just what he needed. It was from the big boss in Omaha. It read, "An oil company in New Zealand is formulating plans for some offshore exploring. We believe that it is time that you go down there and see if we can do some business."

David was eager for yet another change of scenery.

He was looking forward to seeing someplace new and maybe meeting new people. At the Honolulu Airport, he boarded the Quantas Airlines Airbus, and he took pleasure in his new upscale status that gave him first-class accommodations.

He was comfortably seated in his first-class seat, sipping a New Zealand drink, Kraken and Coke, and getting himself into the Kiwi mood. It wasn't the extra luxury that first class provided but the fact that first class catered to mostly successful people, and he was thrilled to be included among them. The pretty flight attendants with the English accents helped his new feeling of sophistication too, with their pampering of first-class passengers.

On the long flight, he began to think about himself, something he learned to do in college psychology. He knew in his guts that he was a coach-class passenger and should be back there with the rest of them, with his knees in his face and eating bland airline food instead of eating filet mignon and sipping the best wines and stretching his legs out full length. But again he knew that he was a liberal working- guy kind of person. He, just like every liberal working-class person, really enjoyed the luxuries that were thrust on him. But in his gut, he was for the little guy and, in fact, hated when they were treated unfairly. He also had learned that that feeling had little to do with success in business. Or so he thought.

It was a long trip, and his thinking went even deeper. He thought about himself and Julia. He realized that people loved one another for a reason, and he wondered why he had loved Julia so much. It was beyond the obvious that she was a very pretty girl. She wasn't particularly kind, and she wasn't particularly loving or even that much fun. She was too self-centered and conceited to get her mind off herself and have some genuine fun and interest in others. For example, it would be no joke they could laugh at if her makeup was misapplied in any way, no giggles over running mascara. In fact, that was all such serious business that he would incur her wrath if he tried to kid her about it. The only conclusion that he could come up with was that he wanted her above all reason. All he knew and could be sure of was that she was his first love, and he had loved her deeply. He had no other experience with women with which to compare her, so he was stuck with his own observations. In truth, he cared nothing about other girls anyway. His one and only interest was with Julia.

When the Airbus landed with a chirp of rubber, a thump, and the roar of reverse-thrusting jet engines, his eyes were at the window. They had landed in Auckland, the main city on the North Island. New

Zealand, he had learned, was made up of two main islands, North Island and South Island. But all he could see, of course, were the activities of a modern airport.

It wasn't until he was in his limo en route to the New Zealand oil company's main office outside of Auckland did he start to notice the distinct flora. He saw ancient evergreens, which the limo driver told him were many millions of years old. There were also shrublands and grasslands interspersed. It was nothing like the States or Hawaii. Whereas the Hawaiians were very diverse, ranging from Filipino to Chinese, the native people of New Zealand, called Maoris, were a homogenous Polynesian people with unique characteristics.

At New Zealand Oil, a very attractive receptionist with a short blond bob greeted him. She was about twenty-five, and her name tag read "Pam." As soon as she spoke, she suggested class. In the States, she would be very much in vogue, as secretaries with that cultivated English accent were all the rage. She eyed him up and down. Though she was smiling, her green eyes didn't catch up with the smile on her lips. Though she was a beautiful girl, there was something oddly sad about her. "Welcome to New Zealand Oil. I'm Pam, may I help you?"

"David March. I think you're expecting me."

"Oh yes. The company doesn't get many Hawaii visitors. It'll just be a few minutes while we gather the players. Is this your first time in New Zealand? Oh, I'm sure you've been all over the world."

"Nope, no world traveler. Yeah, it is my first visit to New Zealand. I hope I can see some of the country."

"So you're from Hawaii," she said almost wistfully. "I wish I could afford a vacation there! It sounds so… so bloody romantic. I don't think I know anybody who has been to Hawaii—at least, any girls my age."

A buzzer interrupted their conversation.

"They are waiting for you." She turned back to him. "If you will follow me, I'll show you to the conference room."

In the conference room, David was introduced to everyone and had just a little trouble understanding their New Zealand accent, which was a mix between Aussie and English with a bit of UK dialects thrown in.

There was a general discussion of the company's expectations and their hopes of renewing an old well. David was no wildcatter, but he had developed what the old-timers considered a nose for oil. He could smell it. Of course, the New Zealand company would need the most up-to-date, cutting-edge technology to have any chance. His nose for oil was all superstition, but lots of fortunes were made on the same kinds of instincts. David not only knew his oil-drilling equipment, but he also knew his geology.

The CEO of New Zealand Oil said, "David, in the morning we'll let you head out and take a look at our equipment and give you a chance to see some of the countryside." Turning to Pam, who was taking notes, he asked, "Pam, will you ride along with David and show him to the hotel later?" He didn't make it sound like a friendly request but like an order, and she agreed to his request as if it were.

She said, "Of course, sir."

David headed right to his room and, after a light dinner, turned in in order to recuperate from the jet lag. Pam arrived on schedule in the morning in the company limo. She seemed even more beautiful in the sunshine, the green eyes taking on a glacial affect. She had coffee and some sort of New Zealand pastry that looked and tasted something like apple strudel. They breakfasted while the limo headed out to the site. Evidently, it was quite a way out. As David gazed out at the countryside, questions came to mind. The first thing he said was "I see the name kiwi on everything. Kiwi Pub. Kiwi Hotel."

She grinned. "Unlike your majestic and imperious American eagle, the kiwi is an unpretentious fat little bird who can't even fly. And that is the icon and the nickname for New Zealanders. We're like that unpretentious fat little bird. We don't expect too much, but we're always hopeful."

They shared a chuckle over that. He said, "My education is technical, and I know little about the world as yet. But what do you folks think of Americans?"

She gave that some careful consideration before saying, "I'd say, the New Zealand history is a lot like you Yanks. We're a far-off land settled by English- speaking people—the British, Irish, Welsh, Scots. We're much that same. We are more or less politically and culturally in step with the United Kingdom and America in general, except for our almost zealous abhorrence of nuclear power. Whenever a nuclear Yank ship comes into the harbor, it raises all kind of havoc. People find every boat in the harbor and go out and harass them to the point that the police become involved."

"So you folks would rather that the bad guys have nukes and you don't? Doesn't that pretty much put you at their mercy?"

"Yeah, that's true."

"I see there are black people here too," David said.

"They're not Africans. They're a Polynesian people called Maoris and are much like any other Polynesian islanders. They're a simple, generous, peaceful people who have been badly treated in the past. Their history is much like your own American experience. You know, their lands invaded by English-speaking newcomers."

"Are there racial problems?"

"Oh yes, at first. But today there have been many reforms made, and there are improvements. Of course you can't legislate how people should feel about other people. You can't legislate what the heart feels or wants to feel. Change can only come with a change of heart and time."

"How about your own family? How did they wind up here?"

She gave this even more thought. "Well, me great-great-granddad came to the South Island back in the 1860s for the gold rush."

"Wow, you guys had a gold rush back about the same time we did."

"Ya, that's true," she said in her charming accent. "Ya, he was actually running from the Welsh police, so New Zealand is about as far away from Wales as one can run."

Even with all this charming, interesting talk, there remained that lingering bit of sadness in her beautiful green eyes.

"So tell me about Hawaii," she said. "All I know about it is the poster on the wall in the break room."

"Heck, I'm just a hick from Omaha." "Omaha?"

"Yeah, it's in Nebraska. We grow wheat. The most exciting thing to do on a Saturday night is watch the bumpers on cars rust." She offered a blank look.

He laughed. "I'm sorry. But I've only been in Hawaii a short while, and I still have a lot to learn about it. I can tell you it is beautiful with no exaggeration. I keep forgetting that here in New Zealand, I'm in a totally foreign country. Hawaii is an American state, and you can get anything from a Coke to a Big Mac. The big difference—it is an island paradise. Gorgeous beaches, soft breezes, and a delightful climate, most of the times. It does have a rainy season in the winter.

"I got transferred there and I jumped at it. I had just come off a bad romantic experience, and I was ready for something new and different. Besides, who could resist an offer to work in Hawaii?"

She was quiet for a while. Finally she said, "At least you found yourself an escape."

The comment begged a question, but he didn't feel he knew her well enough to ask it. Instead he kept the conversation going on general mutual topics.

David noticed no ring on Pam's finger. Searching for clues as to her romantic status, he innocently said, "I hope your boyfriend doesn't mind you riding around the countryside with strange men."

Pam grinned. "I just pal around with casual friends these days. Nobody serious for me at the moment."

At the site, David made a thorough examination of the equipment. He went from wellhead to wellhead, examining everything, his keen and practiced eye missing nothing. At one point, a green lizard skittered across the well platform, and David, startled, jumped.

His guide chuckled, "Nothing to be worried about, mate. It's a gecko." "Gecko?"

"Yeah, I think you got them little—whatcha call 'em—Komodo dragons? They look pretty much like them."

After a long day, David and Pam were back in her office, unwinding. The staff was leaving. David asked her, "What do you do for excitement in the evening?" "Them that have money can do the nightclubs. The others just hang out. Well, if you can afford it, all the best nightclubs and discos are on Princess West Street downtown. There's a lot of variety. Or you could go to a pub, a movie, or as I said, if you can afford it, to one of the fancy nightclubs like Bungalow 8 or the Deluxe Club or Aesha or a number of others."

"Do you go to nightclubs often?"

"Yikes. Oh no, the most I could do is an occasional movie or a visit to the pub. As I said, the best nightclubs are way too expensive for ordinary working people. It would cost me a week's pay. I have to support meself, me mum, and me grandmum. Dad's been gone quite a while now."

David grinned. "If you would like to go to a nightclub with me, I'd be honored. It would be all on me. Whaddya say?"

She hesitated.

He said, "You can't turn down a rich American. I bet the company has rules against that."

Pam smiled widely. "I'd love to go. You do need a reservation, but of course, I would be happy to make one."

"What do you say you make the reservations in my name?"

David realized that he was playing a role, that of the big-shot American. But it was fun. He made it a point that, when he picked her up at eight, he used a car service rather than a taxi. It was obvious, when she came out of her modest apartment, that she was impressed. When they arrived, there was a crowd of very beautiful, very hip young people crowded around the entrance of the Kiwi Club.

Since it was so different than nightspots in Omaha, David asked, "Why are all these people just standing around? This place somewhat reminds me of the nightclub scenes in the old movies of the forties."

Pam said, "When the doors open, we all go in and are seated at the same time. On our tickets, it shows we ordered a five-course dinner. Everyone gets served at the same time."

While there wasn't much that was exclusive about the club that warranted the high price, the energy that flowed through the place made it seem like the epicenter of a major storm and, therefore, worth it.

When they had entered, a waiter took their ticket and said, "Table seven, follow me, please."

Pam said, "That's us."

A waiter escorted them to a long table with ten place settings on both sides. Everyone took their seats and ordered drinks. Pam introduced him to the latest Kiwi drinks. They all had some kind of fruit base.

She looked around the table and said, "Let's meet our dining partners." They got up and milled around, everyone introducing themselves, David sometimes having trouble with the names spoken in the New Zealand accent. But most of the New Zealanders recognized his American accent.

The drinks arrived, and shortly, the first course was served. After the first course, the orchestra began to play. Everyone at the table got up and made a beeline to the dance floor. David asked Pam for a dance, and she eagerly accepted. They headed out to the floor. The music ranged from the latest stateside stuff to the old-fashioned favorites.

As they were dancing, Pam said, "So what do you think so far? Nice place but be honest."

David nodded and said, "Pam, I'd be happy anywhere I was with you. You impress me a lot more than the club."

She smiled, and he could almost detect a blush on her porcelain skin. He concluded that maybe Pam was a country girl new to the big city and only recently becoming sophisticated. He chuckled to himself—as if he himself were sophisticated.

As the second course was served, the dance floor emptied.

She was very attentive to him, helping him pick out the unfamiliar dishes. At one point, when her napkin slid off her lap, David reached down to pick it up.

Pam inquired, "What are you doing?"

"You dropped your napkin. I'm getting it for you."

The men erupted in laughter. The women, in various stages of outrageous laughter, tried to stifle the embarrassment.

Pam cupped her hand and whispered into his ear, "In this country, what I just dropped is called a serviette. A napkin is—well, a napkin is—how should I put this? Well, it's what we use for feminine hygiene."

David sat up quickly and, in a loud voice, said "Oh, Pam, you lost your serviette," which brought another round of laugher.

He got a lot of good-natured cheers for that, and someone called out, "Buy the Yank a drink for being such a good sport!" Then there was a heartfelt hip, hip, hooray in his honor, and he joined in the good spirits.

David and Pam got out on the dance floor, and David was using all his best moves as Pam did her best to follow his American style, which wasn't all that distinct. "You Yanks dance a mean set, don't you?"

They went back to their table for the next course.

After the last course and a couple more drinks and a couple more dance sets, Pam said, "Well, that was the last course. We can leave or stay and enjoy the music. The management leaves it up to us."

"I'll let you make the call."

"To be honest, David, like I said, I don't get to do this very often, so if you don't mind, I'd like to stay."

"Stay we shall, then."

David had had a wonderful time. Back at her apartment, he walked her to the door and gave her a friendly peck on the cheek, but she yanked him to her by his tie and pressed her lips to his, giving him a deep, passionate kiss, her lips soft and moist.

"Don't want you to forget me too quick," she said with a grin. "How often does a working Kiwi girl meet a rich Yank who is a good kisser?"

"The good-kisser part is news to me, but coming from you, I consider it a compliment," he said, feigning a kind of ultra charm. "No chance I'll forget you." He got in the car and was off, feeling very satisfied—not only with the evening but also with his newfound sophistication. At least there were people in the world to whom he was sophisticated.

David stayed in Auckland for a week and spent another week at one of the company's sites on the South Island. Whenever he called into the main office in Auckland, he managed to speak to Pam, who was as friendly as ever. She also seemed eager to know when he was getting back to Auckland.

At the end of his stay, he said good-bye to his new colleagues and took Pam over into a corner to say a personal good-bye. She avoided any impropriety on business premises but murmured to him, "I hope we can keep in touch. I had a wonderful time while you were here. I'm going to miss you." She slid a card into his hand. "It's my phone number. When you feel the need to talk to a friend, call me."

If nothing else, Pam let him know that there were other women in the world who might appreciate him. Julia might have been the one who got away, but girls like Pam were worth pursuing. He thought about her during most of the long flight back to Hawaii. In some of his thinking, he compared her to Julia; otherwise he just thought about her.

One day months later, David was busy at work when he received two letters in the mail. His mail was usually very official looking, but these letters had handwritten addresses and US postal stamps. One was from his mother. In part, it read, "I saw Julia in town today, carrying a baby. I stopped and talked to her. It's a girl. She named it Ashley. The word around town is that she and her husband have separated."

He couldn't figure out how he felt about that, and frankly, he didn't want to try. How embarrassing it would be to go looking her up. She would probably give him the same treatment she did in high school. No, those days were over. His psyche couldn't take any more disappointment.

The other letter was from Pam. It read, "Hi, David. Great news. I have accepted a position in London. When I leave, I will be sailing on a P&O liner Oronsay. Before I make any final arrangements, is your offer to stop by for a visit still good?"

David smiled and reached for his phone.

His heart was full of joy as he waited by the Aloha Tower at the Port Authority for the Oronsay inbound from New Zealand. He spotted her on the fantail, the wind wrapping her dress around her long legs.

She was waving madly, and when he met her at the debarkation gate, she almost bowled him over as she threw herself into his arms. He had a Hawaiian lei for her, made up of a bunch of flowers. "Strictly native Hawaiian, from the orchids to the hibiscus. Aloha," he said and kissed her eager lips. Then he slipped the lei over her neck as a band on the dock played Hawaiian music and hula girls swayed their hips, making their grass skirts shimmy.

"Promise you'll tell me if I stay too long. Is thirty days too long?"

He kissed her lips. "Not long enough, darling. Not hardly long enough."

They spent the first night at a hotel. She bubbled over with enthusiasm about seeing David. When they made love, he felt very familiar with her even though they had only had sex twice while he was in New Zealand.

He took her to a place near Diamond Head for dinner. "No visit to the islands, in my opinion, should start in Honolulu. So in the morning, we're going to take a puddle jumper over to Maui. I feel that's the best place to start a Hawaiian trip."

She turned to him. "A puddle what?"

He laughed. "A puddle jumper. A small plane. Are you afraid of small planes?" She hugged his arm. "Not if I'm with you."

He couldn't tell if she was being a good sport or if she really wasn't afraid. Later as they walked the sands of Waikiki, he stopped, took her into his arms, and kissed her. There was more longing in the kiss than he had expected. It wasn't that he knew her that well, but she had been the only serious romantic interest in his life in a long time.

In the morning they took a twin-engine DeHaviland Otter over to Maui and landed at the airport in Hana. He noticed that she seemed to hold his hand extra- tight. He knew she was afraid but was making the effort for him, and that pleased him as it was pretty much a new experience.

On Maui, they rented a jeep and set out westbound on the road to Maalea Bay on the south coast. It was no superhighway by any means, and it was a bit of a challenge navigating it. The breeze whipped her hair straight back, and with the open top, the sun beat on them. He said, "I never even asked you. Do you snorkel or kayak?"

"I'm a new hand at kayaking, but what Kiwi girl wouldn't know how to dive?" "Would you like to?"

"Absolutely."

As soon as they were ten or so miles west of the airport, the land to the right, opposite the ocean, began to rise until they were looking up at thousands of feet of green mountainside. On the left side between the hilly parts, fields of sugarcane and pineapple stretched away to the horizon. Workers cutting the cane and the pineapples stopped to wave at them.

Gazing seaward, she muttered, "Magnificent! Absolutely amazing!"

It was late in the day when they reached Maalea Bay, and so they rented a cottage on the seaside in time for a sunset dinner—simple fare of local fish, hot fresh-baked bread, and pineapple.

During the afternoon, David learned more about her and she about him. He left out the stuff about Julia. She didn't seem to want to go into old boyfriends either but was happy telling him about her family and her life in New Zealand. Both seemed a bit cautious in revealing their past, possibly because neither felt that they were not that deep into the relationship—yet.

After dinner, they sat out on the veranda and watched the huge yellow orb drop into the whitecapped sea.

When she came in after her shower, a towel wrapped around her, he had no doubt about her intentions when she dropped the towel. After they made love that night, she clung to him. He liked being needed. He knew what it felt like to be needy but not the other way around.

In the morning, they went down to the local dock and hired a kayak. They were told that the bay was usually calm and peaceful but to head back in if they saw stormclouds. They first paddled around the shore, never more than a hundred yards off the beach. They'd paddle for a while and then just drift lazily, letting the tide take them wherever it went. Pam had been wise enough to purchase a basket lunch at the nearby restaurant, and at lunchtime, they found a secluded cove and paddled the kayak up onto a spit of sand that stuck out.

Both had developed an appetite from all the paddling. David pulled his watertight bag out from the forward compartment of the kayak and stretched a blanket out. They lunched on deli sandwiches, pickles, potato salad, and red wine.

Right after lunch, Pam was already out of her shirt and Bermuda shorts. It wasn't the first time he'd seen a lot of her skin, but it was always in dimly lit bedrooms. In the dazzling sunlight, she was spectacular. Long tanned legs, sleek body—stretched out on her back, she was a goddess in a lime-green bikini. He leaned over her and nibbled her lips.

"I always heard from the old folks that the Yanks were pushy." She giggled and pushed him away.

After lunch, they pulled the blanket up into the shade of some coconut palms and dozed off.

It was midafternoon when they awoke. "Try some snorkeling?" he asked.

She was all for it, and moments later, they were out near a reef, cruising along, looking at the sea life beneath them. When they came up, David said, "I'm told you can see over a hundred and fifty feet in this water. Probably the clearest water in the world, I understand."

"I believe it. I recognized almost all kinds of fish. Some we don't have in New Zealand."

Before they left Maui, they had their fill of snorkeling and kayaking, and they even learned to windsurf. Both took quite a few dunkings before they got the hang of it, but when they did, they were skimming the waves like pros, the breeze in their faces, drying them off from the dunkings. When they raced each other, Pam had learned the trick of coming up alongside another surfer 's sail, thus stealing the wind and causing the other sail to slacken enough for her to get ahead.

"Pretty sneaky," he said laughing.

David said later, "You mentioned old folks. What old folks?"

"Me granddad and grandmum. They remembered the marines overrunning Auckland during the war."

"My grandfather was with the First Marines. They were here in Auckland before they hit Guadalcanal."

"Small world."

There had been something on his mind ever since he had met her. And he found that at this particular moment, he could wait no longer to ask it. He made eye contact, and when she recognized it, she tried to break it off. He said, rather forcefully, which was uncharacteristic for him, "Don't look away. What is it in those beautiful eyes that looks so sad? What has happened to you? I don't know why, but it seems to me like more than life's usual problems, man troubles, and such."

She was quiet for a while before saying, "I don't know what you see, but it's no more than the usual. Men trouble, money trouble, etc."

He didn't believe her. It wasn't anything that she said, because she was convincing enough. It was something else, and he had a decision to make. Was he just nosy, or did he care enough for this girl to really want to know what made her unhappy? Was he going to ruin what was, so far, a delightful trip because of his curiosity? Or was he going to mind his own business and let it go?

He decided on the former. He took her hand. "Pam, I know it might sound like I'm just a nosy bastard, but the truth is, I do find myself caring for you, and I'm also finding that you looking unhappy sometimes makes me unhappy too. If there's anything I can do to help whatever your problem is, please consider me a friend and let me help. That is if it is something I can help you with."

A long time went by before she spoke. She gazed into his eyes. "Sometimes," she said, "I think if I have to keep the secret one minute longer, I will disintegrate into tiny little particles and blow away in the ocean breeze."

"Then please tell me."

She said, "David, I like you very much. In fact, more than very much. You don't know much about me, but I don't hop into bed with a man I just happen to like or am attracted to. Never in my life have I done that. It is an important thing to me. I'm considered old-fashioned even for New Zealand."

That made him feel wonderful, making his need to know her trouble ever stronger.

"So please tell me."

She got up, went to the tiny fridge, and got a beer. She motioned to him if he wanted one. He nodded yes, and Pam brought back two beers and set one in front of him. She took a sip. "Remember, I told you that me great-great-granddad came here for the gold rush. He hooked up with a beautiful—so I'm told—Maori girl, and so I have Maori ancestry. In other words, I'm partially black."

David's jaw dropped. His face was so flabbergasted that it probably shocked her.

"You're horrified?" she asked.

"Yeah, I am. I'm horrified that you'd let something as trivial as that upset you to the point of making you look perpetually sad."

"You don't understand."

"I think I do. You are prejudiced."

For the first time, he saw her get mad. Her cheeks flamed red. Her green eyes fairly snapped with rage. "Don't you see? My job helps support not only me but also me mum and grandmum. Without it, we're all on the dole, and I swear I will not be on the dole."

"I understand that, but I think that's all I understand."

"In these days of 9/11, they are checking out everybody. And I mean everybody. Although my ancestry probably can't legally get me fired, the stigma might. Like I said, this country has made some great strides, but you can't change what's in people's minds and hearts. I have no doubt I'd find myself in the street. That's not in the law, but that's just the way it is. Surely, you know that.

"And the other thing about it is that the Maoris are a fine people. I don't want to have to hide my heritage. Darn it, I want to be proud of it. And in fact, I am. But the lousy world won't let you be who you are. They have to pigeonhole you into some category or other. And some categories aren't slated for good things. The Maori have to fight for everything and anything they get in this country."

Another long silence followed. Finally David said, "Look, Pam, I'm sure you know your own people better than I ever will, but I think you're worrying about nothing. And besides, you have friends."

"None that can help me."

"You do now. You have me. I won't let anything terrible happen to you. Not while I'm around."

"You have that much influence?"

"Maybe not right now. But I will, and I promise you, I won't let anything bad happen to you."

She fell into his arms, sobbing. "I always wanted to be an independent person, need nothing from anybody. It's the way I was brought up, and it is something in the Kiwi spirit that is natural to us."

"Pam," he murmured, "please believe me. You have a friend in me."

That night, their lovemaking had a particularly soulful quality to it, and he had never felt so wanted and needed in his life.

Back in Oahu, David treated her to the usual tourist fare—luaus at the Royal Hawaiian, a visit to the Arizona Memorial, a visit to the Polynesian Museum, and climbs up Diamond Head and the National Memorial Cemetery of the Pacific, better known as the Punchbowl.

Before she left, he had one more treat in store for her. He said, "I'm taking you to my favorite watering hole for a drink."

As they pulled into the underground parking at the Reef Hotel, Pam asked, "We're going to have a drink in an underground parking lot? That will be different and something I've never done."

"You guessed it," he said pointing to a sign that read Davy Jones Locker. He said, "This is the place."

She grinned. "Oh, this is a bit more like it. It's very romantic, isn't it?" she said in that English mannerism. After they were seated and having a drink, her glance at the window behind the bar evoked a giggle. The large plate glass window behind the bar was also the wall of the hotel's swimming pool. On the bottom of the ledge where swimmers would stand and adjust their swimsuits, men had no compunction to scratch what needed scratching—as did women sometimes, with an extra flourish. When several swimmers gathered, the waitress would take a stack of free drink cards to the deep end of the pool. She would call all the swimmers to the deep end and yell, "Free drinks at Davy Jones Locker for anyone who takes off their bathing-suit bottom and waves it over their head!" And there was the real show, sort of a takeoff on reality TV. Pam, a naturally conservative girl and not the bawdy type, found that she couldn't hold it any longer and let out a rip-roaring laugh.

He said, "Guess what, Pam? You're already seeing the show. Anyone who takes off their bathing-suit bottom and waves it above their heads gets a free drink. It's a strange thing to do for a free drink, but by the time they're ready to do it, they are already three sheets to the wind."

She looked puzzled. He said, "Loaded."

Pam was blushing now as several people started waving their bathing suits around. There was an abundance of scissoring legs, both male and female. She said, "Nobody will believe this when I tell them. I guess it wasn't very romantic. You Yanks are a bawdy bunch, aren't you?"

It was time for her to leave, and David was seeing Pam off on her trip to London.

She said, "Has thirty days ever passed quicker?"

He hugged her around the waist. "You have lots of adventures ahead, adjusting to your new life in London and all."

She gazed at him. "What's your next adventure? It must be a tough job traveling around finding girls to come to Hawaii for a stay."

Lapsing serious, he said, "Believe it or not and putting myself in jeopardy of losing my coolness, I've never had a girl here. From anywhere."

"And I thought you were so sophisticated."

She simply gazed at him, wondering whether to believe him. He thought that she finally did. He said, "I have to go back to Omaha. I've made a reorganizing suggestion, and the home office wants a little more detail."

"Well, when you get back, be sure to be careful of those lazy afternoons at Davy Jones."

He could tell she didn't want to say good-bye. By this time, he was wondering if he was in love with her. Neither of them actually said the words, but they were more than affectionate together—something more than casual lovers so in vogue these days. He almost asked her before she boarded the ship, but he didn't. Her eyes seemed to be asking him too, but she only said, "In my first letter from London, I will better be able to express myself. I'm too confused right now—too many emotions."

"I understand," he said, but he really didn't. If people loved each other, what was so hard about saying it?

CHAPTER FIVE

David had been asked to address the board of directors of Waverly. The subject was the changing oil world. By now, he was becoming an expert in his field and in the field of world oil production. He started. "With changing world exploration, I feel it is no longer cost-effective to maintain our office in Honolulu. South America is a vast new market. I suggest relocating the Honolulu office to San Diego. I've had accounting run the numbers on the annual office expenses and travel expenses. As you know, expenses tend to run high on Hawaii due to the fact that everything has to be imported. Also, you must take into account that our revised quality control procedures have increased our equipment reliability to the point a customer service call can correct a problem rather than having to put a man on-site. The figures show that having an office in San Diego would realize a savings of thirty percent on office expenses and fifty percent on travel." A quiet settled over the room. "This is actually better than it seems because not only will we be saving money on office and operating expenses, but we will also be closer to a new and emerging market in South America and Mexico for that matter."

Now the CEO spoke. "Interesting concept, David. I'll give all departments a week to evaluate your proposal." He then turned to his assistant. "Schedule a department-head meeting for a week from today, at which time a decision will be made. David, if you have nothing urgent on your calendar, I suggest you remain until after the meeting as your further input may be needed."

By the following week, the decision was made, and David was ordered to close down Honolulu and set up a new office in San Diego.
This, he soon found, was a bigger chore than he had anticipated, especially if one was to do it right. Finding the exact right office location was
no simple chore in itself.

For the next several weeks, David was up to his neck with the details
of the move. Shutting down the Honolulu office was relatively easy, but
finding suitable space in San Diego, furnishing it, and finding suitable
personnel were a heavy load. And it all took valuable time, which was
at a premium.

And in the middle of all this, a contract in South America demanded
his immediate attention on-site.

So he had to drop everything and go to Buenos Aires. As he flew
Aerolinea Argentina to Buenos Aires, he had a lot of time to think about
his life. It certainly wasn't routine or ideal, except in some ways.

CHAPTER SIX

I t was another dreary night, the kind that single mom Julia dreaded the most. She missed adult companionship, mostly in the evenings. And it was a chore getting through the evenings on TV and the occasional phone call from friends. All she did mostly was think, and that made her even more bitter about the way her life turned out. She had hoped she could have had the best of two worlds: a husband to support her and her child and girlfriends to play with.

She was sitting by her window, gazing out, thinking about the past. She had just put Ashley to bed, and now, at the loneliest part of her day, she was in a major funk thinking about her life. As far as male companionship, the pickings out there were scarce. Lots of guys didn't want girlfriends with kids. Most of the others were divorced. And they carried their own set of luggage. But most of all, all any of them really wanted, no matter how charming they started out, was to get into her pants.

She reached for a pen and paper and sat down to write to David. She had been putting it off for months.

Dear David,

I talked to your mom, and she told me how wonderful your career is going and gave me your work address. Your mother makes it sound like you are very happy and doing well for yourself. I wish I could say the same. I'm single now and have a beautiful five-year-old daughter

named Ashley. We are now living with Mom and Dad
until I can afford an apartment or get on public housing
for Ashley and me. Public housing would be best because every day I'm around my parents, I feel more and
more like such a loser, such a failure. I know it might
sound like I'm writing just to bitch to you, but believe
me, I'm not. I'm motivated by thoughts of better days.
I'm not writing to depress you although these days I
know I can do that, but I'm writing to try to relive some
of the great high school days.

David was so overwhelmed by the letter that he didn't stop to
think that a lot of their high school days weren't so great. A lot of it
was him fighting with her for her love and attention and her blowing
him off for guys she deemed more cool, but he did have to admit
there were lots of times when they got along great and they seemed
to be a couple.

She wrote,

I'm working to get my life back on track. Life is a great
teacher, and I'm not pleased with the attitude I had. It
now saddens me when I think about our rocky high
school relationship. You went on to rock the world. I,
on the other hand, have hit rock bottom. Ashley is the
one joy I salvaged from the past.

The next time you're back this way, I'd love to see
you now that the rocky road has smoothed out.

Julia

Sometime later, it was another dreary day for Julia, and she was
thinking of calling David. But it was a pride thing. She hated to come
crawling back, but that was exactly what she would be doing. She thought
she had snagged a rich man, but as it turned out, he was just using her for

sex and wound up marrying someone else. With only another moment's thought she then lifted the receiver and again replaced it. Chewing her lip, she now began tugging at her hair.

She finally did it, but it was a couple of months later. Unable to stand it any longer, she had to take a chance. Finally, she took a big breath and dialed a number. When David answered, she said, "Do you recognize a voice from your past?"

David's cheery "Hey, Julia, nice to hear from you" disarmed her a bit. He didn't sound like the shy, awkward kid she had remembered.

She hesitated to say "What's up?" and soon, the years since high school had flown by, and they were chattering away like old times. Of course they, as if by mutual agreement, only talked about the better times. The bitterness, the disappointment, and the unhappiness were left out. The call ended with a promise to get together soon.

That week, David arranged to travel to Omaha. When the cab deposited him at the address Julia had given him, he was surprised. It was in one of Omaha's cheapest projects. Rows and rows of brick buildings with chain-link areas for children's play areas. If he hadn't had an address, one building looked exactly like the next.

As he climbed to the second floor of her building, a faint odor of urine permeated. He was sad and shocked at the same time that the love of his young life was reduced to this. When he knocked on the apartment door, there was absolutely no indication on his face that he was either surprised or disappointed in her surroundings.

Julia was all smiles, and as the evening wore on, they found lots to talk about. She evidently had not planned dinner and put out some crackers and cheese and a cheap bottle of wine. He remembered their high school days and her love of Chinese food, especially hot, crisp moo shu pancakes, so he suggested they order some. This also helped lighten the mood and tension between them.

The chatter between them had been much easier on the phone. They found themselves, at times, fighting an uncomfortable silence.

She showed him her daughter, Ashley, who had already been sleeping for a while, and he had to agree she was a beautiful child. The conversation, however, steered clear of Ashley's father or the circum-stances of Julia's divorce.

When David left, Julia gave him a chaste peck on the cheek, and frankly, he didn't expect more. The whole visit had been an odd experience in itself. The goddess of his youth, the love of his life, was living on welfare and obviously very depressed no matter how happy she tried to seem about seeing him.

David couldn't stay longer than the weekend, so that Sunday afternoon, they took Ashley out in the stroller and treated her to ice cream and a walk in the park.

When it was time for him to leave, the sadness on her face almost brought him to tears. He found himself promising to come back next week. Getting a babysitter, he could see, was a problem, so he got around it by arranging for one of his teenage cousins to babysit for them.

This date went much better. They visited some of their old haunts—the bowling alley, the burger joint, and a few other teenage hangouts. They were surprised to find that some of them were no longer there.

Julia commented, "Funny, isn't it, how nothing stays the same? Here we are, trying to relive our high school days, and half of it is gone already."

CHAPTER SEVEN

The next date, David took Julia to Mario's Restaurant downtown. Mario's was one of the most exclusive restaurants in Omaha, and it was his choice. At least, he wasn't the poor boy she had known. And she knew he wasn't the type who needed to impress a girl just to get her into bed.

His heart was pounding when he picked her up. Ashley was up, and he found himself oddly pleased to see her. They were no sooner outside the door when the formality of their renewed dating flew off somewhere, and they found themselves clinging to each other and holding each other tightly in the faintly urine-smelling hallway. Julia was clear-eyed when they came apart. She said, "Sorry, I guess my emotions just got the best of me. It's been so great seeing you again all last week and the week before. I was wondering if I hadn't been dreaming and that we hadn't actually seen each other."

In the car, they again clung to each other, and he was intoxicated with the fresh smell of her hair. It smelled like shampoo and sunshine and was so refreshing from the awful smell of the project hallway. They clung together so long in the car that when they broke it off, neither could remember how long it had been.

They found that they were both pretty different from high school. Life had done a number on both of them, and it all wasn't good although David was in a much better place than Julia. Yet all this was bringing David back to a melancholy he hadn't even felt when he was at his lowest about her.

This older, more mature Julia, although a bit world-weary, carried a certain sense of sophistication that was new. He had remembered the flighty, flirty schoolgirl. She was no longer the ponytailed schoolgirl but a modern, hip young woman. One he hoped who realized her mistakes. At least that's what he wanted to think. Before the date, he had convinced himself it wasn't just all a matter of saving face, of not wussing out, but that was as momentary as the moment. Soon they were having a wonderful time, and the conversation had little to do with high school or saving face.

The dating was a unique thing. While he knew her years ago, he didn't know her now. He didn't know what things she liked, what she hated. After all, every high school girl he had ever known was only into the usual things: boys, boys, and boys—except he didn't know the real Julia preferred the soft lips of a woman, the excitement in her breasts.

This Julia was a mother, had been divorced, was more worldly. It was like discovering a new person all over again. After all, the things they had done in high school had little or no bearing on their lives today.

Getting to know Ashley was a wonderful experience for him. He never had any experience with children, having had no siblings of his own. It gave him a warm feeling, and he loved the little hug and goodnight kiss that Julia had taught Ashley especially for him.

Meeting classmates was a rather awkward exchange, and Julia usually whisked him away, not very interested in the old crowd. It was as though she was taking no chances of another girl snatching him up.

His office sent him to Omaha for a one-week assignment. He decided to surprise her and just show up at her place on a Monday night with a dozen roses and a bottle of good wine. When he got to the door, soft romantic music was coming from the apartment, and he knocked on the door. It took a while, but eventually, Julia appeared. The apartment was smoky with pot smoke, and at least three women were there, chattering away, obviously keeping it down now that he was there. Julia, wide-eyed, said, "David! What are you doing here on a Monday night? You never called."

He felt a little foolish, like a kid making up excuses, but he said, "I thought I'd surprise you."

With a tepid grin, she said, "That sure worked. I'm so sorry. I have some girlfriends over, and we were just kind of having a hen party."

David said, "Julia, it's my fault. I should have called, but please take these." He handed her the flowers and the wine. "I'll call you tomorrow. I'm going to be in town all week."

She said, "That's great. Wonderful news. And again, I'm sorry. I'd invite you in, but you'd find a lot of female chatter boring, I'm sure." The way she said it, he didn't even entertain the idea of joining her little party.

The rest of the week went fine. They had more time to spend together even though he was working. They took Ashley to several kiddie places that featured fast food and ice cream and utilized his cousin for a babysitter and went out several times that week.

Dating a woman with a child was different. He had been putting off taking her off on some romantic trip for that reason. It wasn't easy to find a babysitter for a whole week or more. Then it came to him: take the child with them. It was something he could never afford to do with his own family.

When he proposed a trip to Disney World, Julia was all for it and seemed pleased. That alone made him happy.

He had to admit, it was different. Traveling with a child was a whole new experience for him—from keeping her busy on the long plane ride to getting strollers at Disney and to ordering kiddie meals. But he had to admit, he shared in the child's delight. The way her eyes lit up when Alice from Wonderland and Cinderella approached her—she was intrigued and amazed as she actually was with everything in the park. Her favorite was Fantasyland. And the good thing was, she was off to sleep early every night, leaving them the rest of the evening.

There were a couple of new and odd sensations for both. One was making love for the first time, and the other was sleeping with a child nearby. David found that Julia had to run off to check on Ashley whenever there was a strange sound coming from the room. It was usually over quickly, but it did break the mood of the lovemaking. Once in a while, quite unexpectedly, Ashley would get out of bed and come into her mother's bedroom, crying about one thing or another. David would be shocked and hide himself deep in the covers. It was one of the first light moments of their new relationship when Julia laughed. "She won't bite. She has no idea what we're doing—or were doing. All she wants is to get into bed with me. She's been like that since she was a toddler."

Sex was especially new for David and Julia since they hadn't slept together in high school. In fact, he had still been a virgin, while she was not. She wasn't the needy kind of lover but very athletic in her approach, going at it as if it were a sporting event. His instinct was to be more romantic and try for the surreal, otherworldly moments. He couldn't say he didn't like it. And Julia knew things sexually that he barely had heard of. David played the sophisticate but, frankly, was shocked and felt like a novice.

It was fun when they took a side trip to the ocean and hit the beach at Tampa. He even let her bury him in the sand, which she loved. Then they built a gigantic castle. Ashley cried when the incoming tide wiped it out. He'd take her onto his shoulders and bound around in the surf with her. Then splashing in the surf. When all three came out of the water, they were all slick and shiny wet like a family of seals. There was no question about it—marriage was in the air, and they both were ready for it.

But not everyone was for it. David's mother had deep reservations as did some of his friends. His friend Tommy said, "How could you even think about marrying her after the way she treated you in high school?"

David scoffed it off. "Come on, Tommy, we were all kids then, not knowing what we wanted."

Tommy grimaced. "You sure knew what you wanted. You let that girl make a fool out of you."

The sex with Julia, if he were to analyze it, was not breathtaking, but then he didn't have much to compare it to. All he knew was that the biggest thrill of his life was being with her, being in bed with her, and being intimate with her. The baby was no hindrance. In fact, he liked having a ready-made family.

He wrote to Pam about it, considering her just a good friend to share some good news with. He never thought that he might be hurting her, that she might think that there might have been a future for them.

CHAPTER EIGHT

One weekend afternoon, Julia was out shopping when a knock on the door brought Ashley flying to the door. When David opened it, a good-looking man was standing there, and Ashley flew to him. "Daddy, Daddy! You said you were coming before. You promised, you promised. Where were you? I waited and I waited but you never came. You busted me, Dad."

Both men looked at her. Daddy said, "I busted you, honey? What do you mean? I don't understand."

"You busted my heart."

Both adults grinned at that, only Ashley didn't see any mirth in it.

David stood there, a bit stunned as the man scooped up the child and started talking baby talk to her and making all kinds of new promises. All of which caught David unprepared. The man might have been the local pedophile for all he knew.

When Dad finally put Ashley down, who continued to cling to his pant leg, the man stuck his hand out. "I'm Frank Philpin, Ashe's dad. You must be the new man in Julia's life."

David muttered something that confirmed his guess, but somehow it left him feeling a bit foolish.

Philpin said, "When do you expect Julia back?"

David honestly said, "I'm not really sure since I don't know where she went. She said something about shopping, but she often visits friends while she's got a babysitter."

"Oh yeah," he said, in a tone that left David completely puzzled. It was just short of rolling his eyes.

"Well, I'm sorry to have to stick around. I can't really go because I have to be out of town on a business trip as soon as I see Julia and settle something with her." Somehow the comment and, mostly, his appearance, in an odd way, sent David back a few years. Ashley said, "Daddy, I'm going to show you some of my new toys that Mommy and David brought me. You wait right here. Don't go away!" she admonished waving one of her tiny fingers at him.

While Ashley was rummaging around her room, Phil sat quietly. It was awkward. Finally he said, "So you dig Julia's uh... thing."

David looked genuinely confused. "Thing?"

"Yeah, you know. Her girlfriends. You must have run into them by now. Christ, I used to be knee-deep in them."

"Oh yeah, I've met a few of them. I guess it's a few of them." "Well, you know, some guys dig that."

"Dig what?" David said innocently.

"Come on, man, you know what I mean. Hey, I have to admit, at first, she got me into a few kinky scenes that I didn't mind." Another awkward silence. "In fact, I really dug it. Why, there was this one blonde, I don't know if she's still around. I think her name was... What was it? Oh yeah, Beth. Man! Sheee... Well, let's just say that it was fun until it became everything to her. I was just an accessory. Why I—"

Just then, Julia popped in. Her eyes ratcheted from David to Phil and back. She looked tense. She made sure that she made quick work of Phil's business, and very soon, they were saying their good-byes.

When Phil left, Julia made sure that the topics quickly turned to other things, but when David was alone, he wondered what Phil was talking about.

So he brought it up a few nights later while they were dining at Mario's. Julia waved her hand and said, "Phil is so full of crap—any excuse to say that it was all my fault. Sure, I spent time with my friends, but so did he. He had his bowling night, his pool night, his card night. I didn't bitch about that. Yet I have a few friends over and all of a sudden I'm neglecting him. Anything to make it my fault."

It made sense to David, but when he got to thinking about it, a conclusion came to mind. Maybe these girls all sat around and watched porn. Maybe that's all it was. And he was just being vivid about it and making it more than it was. It made sense to David, especially since he wanted so much for it to make sense. Julia had a way of quickly burying the subject so that it retreated to the back of his mind. She did this with exciting, new, pleasant things for them to do. Even if it lingered there awhile, for now, it was gone.

CHAPTER NINE

Within three short months, David and Julia were married in San Diego. There was no choice about that since that's where David's job was. Julia would come up with alternatives in the future, but for now, they were to live in California and as a ready-made family living the upscale suburban life of the upper middle class. He was glad that his parents seemed to accept it, not that that would have stopped him. They seemed to feel it was inevitable, considering the way he obviously felt about the girl.

Julia did seem to have a problem about leaving her friends behind. The way she explained it was, "I had nobody for so long, my girlfriends were like everything to me. You have to know how lonely I was."

David thought, You're preaching to the choir there, babe.

And nobody could resist Ashley. She was an adorable child. When David's mother commented that she reminded her of Shirley Temple, nobody commented. Nobody in the room went back that far except a few old-timers who nodded their heads in agreement.

Everyone thought that Ashley was the hit of the wedding and that she made an adorable flower girl, and it was a very happy wedding party.

Living in California, which David thought would make Julia very happy, had just the opposite effect. She seemed to really lament the loss of her girlfriends in Omaha, but he was sure that once immersed in the California lifestyle, all that would change. Who would prefer the nasty, mean Nebraska winters to the golden, sun-filled days of Southern California?

He remembered an incident after high school when they took jobs in Omaha. David rented a one-bedroom apartment, and Julia still lived at home and drove to Omaha to work. Due to crop failures, John's rented farm fell on hard times, and he had trouble making the rent payments. Hazel took a job in retail in Omaha.

One severe winter blizzard, the roads were blocked. David, at work, got a call from Julia saying that when it started snowing, she left work and went home. "David, would you do me a favor? Mom can't get home. Could you pick her up and take her to your place?"

David said, "Sure, my four-wheeler can get through anything."

It was a cold, wet blizzard, and by the time he got Hazel to his place, both were soaked with the wet snow-and-rain combination. He went to his closet and got her his robe. "I'll get your clothes into the dryer as soon as I change into dry clothes."

She said, "Meanwhile I'll make us whatever you have—coffee, hot chocolate?" He said, "Both, second shelf."

Later, as they were thawing out, her robe caught on a chair and it flew open, and David was treated to an eyeful of feminine perfection— perfect flared hips, large erect breasts, and long, sleek legs. She seemed unaware of just how beautiful she was, and it was that mature beauty that had something the young ones didn't. It wasn't that the younger ones weren't firmer and more toned, but there was something about a mature woman, the way her thighs filled out just a bit more than the young ones. Even gravity's effect on the breasts of a mature woman was alluring. Who said small, tight, and perky was everything?

She cried, "Yipes, I'm so sorry, David."

David, still wide-eyed, said, "Hazel, you've got nothing to be sorry for. I'm afraid my eyes haven't caught up with my imagination yet, but someone as gorgeous as you shouldn't ever apologize. If anyone should be sorry, it's me for embarrassing you."

"I'm still sorry."

Grinning, David said, "Nothing to be sorry about, Hazel, you're a good-looking woman. Look, my robe obviously doesn't fit, so I'll get you a pair of my pajamas. They should be safe."

When she emerged in his pajamas, he giggled. "This can be our private little joke about the time you got into my pants."

They shared a good-natured but mostly intimate secret and a good laugh, and there was something beyond intimate about it.

She said nothing but simply dropped her head. Lowering her eyes demurely, she said, "Do you think I'm attractive, really?"

"Are you kidding?"

"No, I… I had a hard time when I was a kid."

That piqued David's interest, and he said, "What do you mean?"

"You really want to hear it?" "Yeah, I do."

"Well," she paused, "no, you don't want to hear it."

"To me, what that translates into is that you don't want to tell me." She lapsed quiet again. "Okay, if you really want to hear it."

David sat back and prepared to listen.

She said, "Everyone told me when I was a kid how pretty I was. Well, that sounded good until I started to get a lot of unwanted advances, if you know what I mean. Boys were always gawking at me, and to tell you the truth, the girls weren't very nice to me either."

David nodded. "Jealous."

"Anyway, I got boobs younger than most girls, and that didn't help at all." His glance went to her chest.

She said, "I know, big boobs at that. I had to wear loose, flowing clothes to avoid the comments. You'd think it would be every girl's wish, but believe me, it was no fun. I read a history book once that told about World War II. When the Russians began winning and were closing in on Berlin, the German women made themselves as ugly and shapeless as possible to avoid rape."

"Did it help?"

"Some. There were lots of pretty girls, so the dumpy ones were by-passed. That's what I felt like.

"So as a pretty farm girl, I attracted a lot of attention in a small country high school. One winter day, I had to stay after school to help on a Christmas pageant project. Well, there was this one boy—he was more aggressive than the rest. A lot of them just stared but said little.

This one, Billy Connor, was always making lewd comments and trying to sneak feels. Well, anyway, on the way home from school—it was already getting dark—he appeared from behind a tree and approached me. I was scared to death. He kept saying, 'Come on, Hazel, I know girls like you. You want to give it up but are afraid of what people will say. Well, I won't tell nobody, promise. Come on, we can go in Old Man Cruller's supply shack there. Nobody will ever know.' I didn't want to go anywhere with the likes of him.

"I tried to act brave, but of course, I wasn't. I told him, 'No, Billy. Leave me alone or I'll tell everybody what you tried to do.'

"He was wearing a smirk now. 'No, you won't. You would be too embarrassed.'

"I wouldn't admit it, but he was right. Still, I wasn't going to let him have his way with me. He grabbed me and we struggled. He dragged me into the shack and tore my dress top off. As soon as he saw my boobs, he began pawing me. I didn't know what to do. He was bigger and stronger than me."

David's eyes were bulging. "Christ, Hazel, what happened?"

"Well, he pushed me down on a straw pile and climbed on me, but he wasn't able to get my pants off. I fought like a wildcat. When I kneed him in the balls, he folded, his face red, and he was madder than ever. I grabbed a pitchfork that was hanging on the wall, and I threatened him with it. While I tucked my torn dress top under my coat, I took the pitchfork with me. I said, 'If you come near me, I'm gonna stick you good, Billy.' I guess he saw the anger in my eyes and believed I'd do it.

"By then, all the fight was out of him."

David almost felt like crying; the story was so sad.

Their eyes locked and explored each other. If she were anyone else, he would have hit on her right then and there. But she was Julia's mother. In American tradition, this was taboo. He moved forward, pushing the robe open, and held her close. His plan was to comfort her after the heart-wrenching story, but he kissed her. Their kiss was wet and passionate—probing, exploring, until finally, breathless they parted. David said, "Now it's my turn to be sorry."

"Please don't be. It just happened."

"Because it was an accident or because we both wanted it to happen?" "Either way," she said.

When she went into the guest room, she stared at herself in the mirror for a moment, and eventually, her hand slipped below the pajama waistband, and an abandoned look clouded over her face.

David had to move the family to San Diego, and for some reason, Julia resisted, claiming she didn't like California. But David had to prevail because that's where his work and their great lifestyle required him to go. He purchased a fabulous seaside cliff-top home at Point Loma that had one of the most sweeping ocean views in all of California. Seaside was one thing in any coastal community, but clifftop was a feature that was truly unique. The sunsets were the most spectacular on the West Coast.

They had only been living at Point Loma a few months when Julia suggested, "David, I asked Mom to come out here and spend some time with us since Dad is working out of state. It's awfully lonely for her. I hate to think of her alone every night. I've been through it, and I know how that can be."

David said, "That would be nice. I'll give her a call later and try to convince her to come on out."

He felt a bit guilty saying that, but the problem wasn't that he didn't want her to visit. The problem was that he really did want her to come and visit. He still harbored fantasies about the peep show during the blizzard in Omaha.

A week later, Hazel was walking in their front door, David ahead of her with the luggage. That evening, they were watching Regis Philbin's local TV show, which had Buddy Reed at the piano and Christopher Plummer singing.

Hazel loved that show. She said, "I watch this TV show all the time. All these Hollywood celebrities just walk onstage unannounced, surprising Regis." Like all fanatics, she was earnest about everything in the show.

David commented, "It's just a stop here to hang out awhile on their way to Tijuana for the bullfights, jai alai games, and just—"

Julia interrupted, "Some of the gals are planning a long weekend to San Francisco and asked me to go along. Is that okay with you, David?"

"What's going on in San Fran?"

"They're talking about high tea at the Saint Francis and then touring the Napa Valley."

"Sounds la-di-da." David glanced at Hazel, thinking, What could be better for an out-of-town visitor, but Julia never mentioned it. There seemed to be no doubt that she would not be invited.

Julia turned to her mother. "Mom, is it okay to leave you like this?"

Hazel said, "Oh, go on, we'll have a great time together, I'm sure. There's so much for me to see out here."

Julia brightened.

David thought, As if she really cared what the old girl wanted.

Julia said, "Great, I'll call the gals and tell them to count me in. Thank you, David and Mom."

Just like her, David thought. She brings her mother out here because the old girl's lonely, and what does she do the first chance she gets? She goes off with her pals and leaves her mother. What a sweetheart!

CHAPTER TEN

J ulia was happily packing for her trip. She was never in a better mood
than when she was packing to go somewhere with her gang. David
noticed that her happiest days were when she was going on one of
these hen parties. As he stood in the bedroom and watched her pack,
she said, "David, why don't you see if you can do something special for
Mom over this weekend? She needs to get out of the house."

"I'll be happy to, but I didn't know that entertaining Hazel was
going to be one of my functions."

"Well, I'd take her along, but you know how shy she is, and she
doesn't know any of the girls. The things we talk about would go over
her head. And worse, we would bore her. It's really not her cup of tea."

"Well, okay, I've got some ideas. How do you think she'd like a spa
treatment complete with new wardrobe?"

"That's a great idea. I'll let the girls at the hairdresser and nail salon
know and ask them to treat her well. I know they'll do it for me since
I'm such a good customer at all those places."

After Julia left, David and Hazel dropped Ashley off at the Point
Loma Methodist Church for her weekend church trip. The girl was eager
to go on the trip, so neither adult felt guilty about sending her off.

Both waved good-bye as the bus pulled out, but Ashley was already
busy chatting it up with the other kids.

Hazel asked, "Did Julia ever really say what she was doing this weekend?" "Who knows? She's never really specific about what she does, nor
does she share it with me. Oh, it's just a group of women on a weekend

getaway. High tea at the Saint Francis and the Napa Valley Tours. How about you? Are you ready for a day on the town?"

"Very ready, David."

David found that Hazel wasn't at all the sophisticate her daughter was. A farm girl at heart, she was shy and embarrassed about being pampered in a fancy salon. She and David sat in the car outside the salon as David tried to convince her how much she'd like it. She kept saying that she'd feel like a phony, and out of place at that. Still, a lifelong habit of being ultraconservative wouldn't allow her to indulge herself in such fanciful things. She was really uncomfortable about the whole thing.

Hazel nervously twirled her hair. David said, "Come on, Hazel. You're gonna love it."

"I can't go in there. I've never been to a spa. I'll act like a hick. No, it's too embarrassing."

"Okay, how about this: I'll go in with you. Believe me, nobody will embarrass you. These salons are used to dealing with upscale customers. They would die before they do anything to make you uncomfortable. Besides, they know Julia and will do their very best to treat you right."

"It's not that, David. Like I said, I'm a farm girl. I don't want to look and sound like a hick and embarrass myself."

"Look, Hazel, they're in business. They want your money, your business. They're not going to do anything to offend you. Believe me, that's how it works. Your money is what interests them most, not your background."

It took ten minutes more of arm twisting and cajoling, but with a deep sigh, she finally relented. As they entered, a very attractive older-looking lady greeted them. "Good morning, David, we've been looking forward to this meeting." Glancing at David, she said, "It'll take about three hours."

He drifted around the area, stopped in for a beer, and watched the ballgame to kill time. Then it was back to the salon. When Hazel appeared with an attendant, she not only had a new look but also actually had a new persona. Her hair had been frosted, her makeup applied expertly, her nails professionally manicured. Even in her plain, unfashionable, Midwestern-style JCPenney clothes, she was a different person. Not only did she look different, but she also seemed to carry herself with more confidence. It was an amazing makeover.

She was glowing at the effects and said, "Thank you, David, for convincing me. I know I can be obstinate."

In the car, David said, "While we're on a roll, will you trust me with the clothes boutique? I guarantee you, it will be a nice experience. Not that I know anything about women's fashions, but the people at the boutique do and they can be trusted.

Believe me, they do it every day. They know what they're doing. Besides, it doesn't take much to make you look good, not with that figure."

But still, Hazel did no more than gawk at the clothes salon. Her confidence dried up as quickly as it came. She said, "I don't know how to shop in a place like this, David. Can't we just go to JCPenney's? At least I'm at home there and know how to shop. Please, David."

"Julia will skin me alive if she thought I took you to JCPenney's. That's not for you, that's so… so Nebraska."

Hazel was an appreciative person and felt badly about what she considered giving David a hard time over this. That helped her get her gumption up. She asked, "Do you really think I can do it?"

"Again, I'll go with you. You won't find anybody being anything but supercourteous. Not at their prices. Don't forget, it's Julia's favorite shop. They know we're coming and that you're her mother. Believe me, hell would freeze over before they're anything but great with you."

The owner, a middle-aged lady who looked like she'd been pampered all her life, greeted them with a big smile. "David, and you must be Hazel. So glad to meet you. Please take your time to browse." Hazel and David exchanged confident glances. The owner said, "When you have a question, please ask."

David grinned. He was beginning to enjoy this—his own personal version of the Henry Higgins makeover from the Broadway show My Fair Lady. Hazel was truly morphing into a world-class beauty.

When they emerged, Hazel was wearing most of the new clothes, with her old clothes in bags. The effect was mesmerizing. They left the store laden with armloads of shopping bags and a couple of boxes that were hard to balance with the rest of the load.

In the car, David said, "You look absolutely amazing, Hazel. Nobody back in Nebraska would ever recognize you. They'd think some celebrity had come to town to do a show."

Hazel took a deep breath and said, "I never knew shopping could be such an experience. I'm used to rude clerks who know little or nothing about the clothes they're selling. To sit and sip wine while people bring you out clothes and even model them for you is an experience out of a gothic novel. The whole day has been a lifetime dream. And you putting up with all my silly hesitance and downright stubbornness. How can I ever thank you? I guess I just need more confidence in myself."

David smiled his most charming smile and said, "And the day's not over yet, my dear. We still have the evening, and that's my department. I'm not going to have to convince you about anything."

That night, after David waited for her to dress, when she emerged from her room, he had to gasp. She playfully did a little flourish and he grinned. The clothes did the utmost with her lovely figure. The lady at the shop even said, "It's one thing to try to make some women beautiful, but with this lady, it was very simple. She enhanced everything she tried on."

One saleslady said, "She should be a model. Everything looks great on her."

That night, he too was dressed for a big evening. He was wearing his new gray Armani that Julia had told him set off his eyes. Hazel had trouble keeping her hands off him. She giggled. "You can take the farm out of the farm girl, but you can't take the farm girl out of the farm. No amount of cosmetics is going to give you that natural country look. You already have it—high color, smooth skin, no wrinkles."

As they sat in the Marine Room in La Jolla at a window seat, they had a panoramic view of the vast Pacific. Soft, dim lights cast erotic shadows. The tinkling of a piano and a steady stream of old romantics and show tunes filled the room. They were even up to a little rock and roll, with David leading the way.

He took her hand. Their eyes were lost in each other 's. He said, "I know what you're going to say: you don't know how or what to order. Well, let me take care of that for you. That is, unless you do know what you want to order."

"Don't worry, I'm not going to order chicken-fried steak. But I do want you to order for me. It's more… more…"

"Romantic?" "Yeah."

They both laughed at that.

When Hazel seemed to lapse deep into thought, he asked her, "A penny?"

"Oh," she said, "I was just thinking, I've only seen things like all this in movies and read about them in books. Now I'm actually living them. It's hard to believe that people actually live like this."

When the waiter arrived, David confidently ordered, "For the lady who likes fishing, she'll have the lobster thermidor and a French pâté." Hazel looked at him, full of admiration.

For an after-dinner drink, David ordered Grand Marnier. Hazel took some sips and savored it. Then she turned to him and said, "Wow, this is some good stuff, never had anything like it." She gazed at him. "You're not going to let this evening go by without dancing with me. I feel like Cinderella at the ball. I just have to dance with you. I want to be in your arms. My night wouldn't be complete without that."

They took to the dance floor and soon were receiving admiring glances. One older woman said to her female companion, "She may be a cougar, but I don't blame the guy. She's gorgeous."

David said, "So how does it feel to be Cinderella?"

"Better than you can ever imagine," she said as they whirled around the floor. "And it feels even better to be confident."

Again with his eyes deep into her eyes, he said, "I'm just warming you up. Are you ready for the next stop?"

"Oh my gosh. What else could there be? Oh yes, can I have another one of those Grandma things?"

David laughed. "We'll order another of those Grandma things at our next stop." He looked puzzled. "Oh, you mean Grand Marnier," he said, pronouncing it in the French way, without teasing her about it but exaggerating the French pretense some used.

Later they were seated at the piano bar. Hazel said, "And I thought nothing could top dinner."

"Nothing like a piano bar late at night to put one… uh, in—let's say—the 'best of the best' mood?"

As she gazed about, she spotted a poster that read Buddy Reed. She exclaimed, "That's Regis's piano player!"

"I know. I know Regis is one of your favorites. That's why we're here. I made the arrangements special."

Hazel reached across the table for his hand. "Oh, David, you're the greatest. That's the greatest TV show, with all those Hollywood celebrities that just walk in unannounced and surprise Regis. I just love it, waiting to see who the guests will be. All the singers sure like Buddy."

He took her hand. "Come on, we're going to meet someone."

Her jaw dropped even as her eyes popped. They headed for the piano and Buddy. There's only one stool available, and Hazel took it, with David behind her, his hands on her shoulders. Buddy gave her an admiring and lingering look. He said to her, "And what might the beautiful lady prefer?"

Hazel gave him her choice, and he looked at her all the while he sang it. Her heart was aflutter, and she could barely hide it. He looked directly into her eyes, crooning to her as he sang the melancholy ballad.

They headed back to the dance floor, and she pulled David closer.

At the end of that number, they returned to the piano and continued a lively chatter with Buddy.

She requested a song and said, "Make it long and slow."

They returned to the dance floor. Hazel's allure and her mood were stirring David. He was almost ready to drag her out of there when a commotion drew their attention. There was a drumroll and the announcer, his voice a rising crescendo, said, "Ladies and gentlemen, please welcome

Mr. Christopher Plummer. Will you sing something for us, Chris?" He graciously agreed, and as soon as the crowd quieted down, he began to sing.

Hazel was giddy with excitement. Suddenly, she turned to David and said, "Am I acting like a hick from Nebraska? This is my first time being a great dame. If I get farm girl on you, please slap me out of it."

Hazel listened, enraptured while Plummer was singing his song. She gasped and grabbed David. Her hand landed on his crotch. Feeling his manhood, she closed her hand around it. When Chris was finished singing, Hazel whispered to David, "We need to go somewhere now!" He was about to protest, but she pulled him by the hand, down to the beach.

By the light of a waning moon, they found themselves, shoes in hand, walking the sands of Coronado Beach. When Hazel stopped and turned to him, lust in her eyes, David was ready, and their kiss was deep, wet, and passionate; their tongues had a will of their own. David laid his jacket on the sand, and they sank down to it, too eager for more foreplay. He was frantically unbuckling his belt as she got out of her dress. They clung together and absorbed each other 's feel and scent. David slipped a finger into her wetness, and she murmured, "No, David, my husband is the only man I've ever touched. I have to do this myself." She reached for his manhood, lowered her head, and engulfed him. He gasped.

Their lovemaking was frantic and quick the first time. The second time, David was able to catch his breath, slow down, and take his time and explore every part of Hazel as he varied his rhythm to give her the peak of pleasure. Just as he brought her to the beginning of a climax, he would stop and wait for both of them to get ready for yet another round.

Later she lapsed quiet, and he picked up on it. He reacted with, "You're so quiet. Are you okay?"

He heard a soft, murmuring sob. "No, I'm a wreck. I've never cheated on my husband. I don't know what I'd do if I had to face him right now. Thank God, I don't have to. It was all so... so dreamlike."

He was trying to think of some way to comfort her when she blurted, "How can any woman resist all this romance? Don't get me wrong, I'm not saying it's your fault. Hell, I wanted it so much." She paused a moment. "Somehow, deep down, something tells me that what we did was not only okay but also right. Times like this come only once in a lifetime, and I think we as humans are helpless to ignore them."

He smiled, understanding what she meant and without giving in to his own guilt. It was impossible to stop, simply impossible.

CHAPTER ELEVEN

The finely tuned engine purred so softly that it made the quiet in the car even quieter. Hazel's voice seemed to be enhanced by the quiet. She said, "I've been waiting all my life for this to happen."

Cocking his head, David said, "What? To have sex?"

He didn't hear her response; it was so soft. She realized it and raised her voice an octave. "No, I mean..."

He hesitated. "You've never done oral sex?" He knew he hadn't asked for it or forced her, so he was puzzled. "I... I didn't know it would be traumatic for you. I—"

"Oh no, please, it wasn't your fault. I loved it. It was... it was so thrilling, so exciting. Don't feel anything but good about it." More silence followed. The only sound was the hum of the tires on the road as both people's minds whirled away.

"John and I are old-fashioned about sex. I must say, especially John. The thought of oral sex would never ever occur to him."

David said, "You mean about lips below the tits, right?"

Hazel tried to stifle the laugh as she was still wallowing in guilt but she couldn't. They shared a hearty laugh.

David said, "Now that you've got the hang of it, how about..."

She said "You read my mind," unzipped him, and lowered her head. Soon her head was bobbing at a steady rhythm that kept increasing until David gasped with the enormity of his pleasure.

She said, "David, do you remember our joke the night of the blizzard?" "Yeah, the night you got into my pants."

She said, "Well, tonight you got into my pants." With that, the tension evaporated.

One night a few months later, David came home to a note on a sideboard near the front hall closet.

"Hi, David, I'm with some girlfriends. Ashley is at the babysitter 's. Pick her up and get something for dinner. I'll be home later…"

He was thinking, Her and those darn girlfriends—you'd think they were joined at the hip.

After dinner, David and Ashley found themselves alone, something they were used to. He said, "What's your choice of board games?"

She giggled. "How about just the two of us playing spin the bottle? I can't lose that way."

He frowned. "Don't be naughty. Now pick your poison."

David had a phone call from Mark in Omaha telling him he was going to resign. "Well," Mark said, "I decided it's time for me to go down the road."

David said, "Hell, I thought when you said you were retiring, you were having a set of radials put on your car."

"It's true, David, it's time for me to go. The board will select my replacement at the next meeting. I want to get out of here as soon as possible, and I've suggested that you come back here and fill in until the decision is made."

When Julia got home, David told her about it. "I have to go back to the home office for a few days. My boss is retiring, and I'm going to fill in for him until a new department head is selected."

She asked, "Does that mean you may get the job?"

He smiled. "Well, it's been hinted I may have the inside track." "I hope so. You know I hate California."

"I don't know why with all the women's activities you're always involved with. Won't you miss the old gang? I never know where you'll be off to next."

She rolled her eyes.

David was sitting behind an impressive desk. His nameplate read, International Customer Relations.

The CEO, Mark Madison, entered the office. "David, would you come with me to the boardroom?"

In the boardroom, a formal meeting had been called. Mark started out. "David, the board members like the way you handled the ICR job. They selected you to be the next International Relations Department head." Everyone stood and applauded.

David told Julia, "Julia, I got the job!"

She said, "Great! I'll be leaving as soon as I can."

Before David could get another word out, Julia was on the phone to her mother. "Hi, Mom, it's Julia. David got the job. I've got a favor to ask you. I want to leave now! Today, if I can. Would you consider coming out here and helping David with packing and the move?"

Hazel was squirming in anticipation. "Well, I suppose I could. Will you book me a flight?"

"Sure. I'll be taking Ashley with me, so it will just be you and David. Call David at the office so you can get together and make plans."

Two days later, Hazel and David were in bed, making love. Later, Hazel said, "I love planning."

"Do you think it'll always be this hard?"

With a naughty twinkle in her eyes, she said, "I'll make sure it is."

"They're giving me a month to close up shop in San Diego. I figure it'll take me less than a week."

A week later, they had the entire house packed and in boxes, most sitting in the living room. Both plopped down on sofa chairs. "Whew," Hazel said, "I'm starting to feel as old as I am."

"How can you say that, darling? You keep me young." David stretched out and then said, "Why don't we hit the Jacuzzi one last time before the pool company closes it down?"

Hazel grinned. With a twinkle in her eye, she said, "Oh gee, I can't. I didn't bring my bathing suit."

Grinning himself, David said, "Oh well, I guess I won't wear one either."

Ten minutes later, they were both sitting in the Jacuzzi naked, drinks on the edge of the pool. David lapsed thoughtful. "You know, we still have a couple of weeks before we have to leave. Anything special you want to do as a last fling? I mean anything you want, don't think anything is too much."

She smiled. "We haven't had our last fling yet, darling." When David got quiet, it aroused her womanly instincts. She asked him, "What is it, darling? You rarely get this quiet after lovemaking."

"Oh, I was just wondering." "What?"

"I was wondering what woman would push a woman as beautiful as you on her husband, encourage them to spend a lot of time together. And especially in such a romantic setting."

"Are you trying to make me feel guilty, David?"

"No, not at all. I wouldn't want to stop any more than you. I just can't resist you. It's like some weird obsession."

She tugged at a stray hair. "I have to admit, it's much the same for me. You're like something I just can't do without."

"Maybe that's just because you've been so neglected." "John leaves me wanting for nothing."

"Except what you really need—what you really want."

She lowered her eyes. "I know. You're right. He gives me everything but what I want most, love and affection. Oh, I'm sure he loves me. But in his own 'good farmer, good husband' way."

"So we're back to, why is she pushing us together?"

Hazel said, "I don't know. But do you know something, darling? I really don't care. I want you and I need you, and so I'm being selfish. Can't you think she's just being a good daughter and trying to treat her mother to something nice?"

"Something very nice, I'd say." She jokingly slapped his arm.

He lapsed serious. "No, really, why would she push us together?" He paused for a while. "I know if I asked Ashley, she'd say, 'So that she could be with her dykey friends.'"

Hazel looked puzzled. "Dykey?" "Yeah, gay, lesbian, you know." "Julia has gay friends?"

David slapped his head. "Boy, you can take the country out of the country girl, but you can't take the country girl out of the country."

"Surely, Julia doesn't participate with these… these women. I mean, the things that they do together."

"Says who? I'm her husband and I have certain intuitions, and my intuitions lead me to believe that she's not only into it but also into it like gangbusters."

Hazel seemed to be getting depressed, and that's not what David wanted. He truly wanted to show her one of the best times of her life.

He hesitated. "Ya know, I was thinking, I'd like to finish off this whole makeover thing with a nice little side trip."

"Like where?"

"How about Hawaii?"

She said, "Get out of here! Really? We can do that?"

A week later they were at Davy Jones Locker in Honolulu, laughing at the bare bodies in the pool behind the bar. The image of Pam flitted across David's mind.

CHAPTER TWELVE

Some years had passed and David was home. David was sitting in his den, reading over some business reports, when he heard the door bang shut. He called out, "Ash, is that you?"

She peeked her head into the den. "Yes, it's me."

"From the sound of your tone, I take it the date didn't go well."

"Men," she snarled. "I should say boys." She made the word boys sound even more derisive than the word men. Her complaint was obvious, and in some ways, it was a universal one.

Still, he said, "Care to explain?"

"They buy you a burger and a Coke, and they think they own you. And now that entitles them to get into your pants."

David frowned in a paternal way. "Now, Ash, I don't think it's fair to group all men—or boys as you say—under one umbrella."

Her whiny, petulant tone clear, she said, "The girls all talk about how great sex is. I've never had it, so I don't know. Sometimes I think they're just bragging. But what I've seen so far, it can't be so hot. A lot of panting and pawing and the girl gets nothing out of it but a torn blouse."

David again lapsed paternal. "Just wait. It's not that sex is great with everyone, it isn't. The right guy will come along, and then you'll be telling your girlfriends how great sex is."

At work in the morning, David was talking to Mark Madison, the CEO. Mark said, "The Russians going to try to extract more oil from an old nonproductive field that's been shut down for years. If it's successful, then the possibilities are endless when one considers reopening a lot of old oil fields."

"And?"

"It may be a market for some of our equipment."

Mark said, "Yes, I can see the potential. I think we need to look into it. What's your idea?"

David steepled his fingers and set his chin at the peak. "Well, it'll take too much time to have our Europe-Africa customer service rep do all the legwork required for a new project."

"I see. That only leaves one person with enough experience that I can feel confident in. When can you leave?"

David was a bit late getting home.

He found Julia and Ashley in the study. Trying for the right level of enthusiasm, he gave Julia a light peck on the lips and said, "How would you like to go to Russia?"

Her face went blank. "Russia? Whatever gave you the idea that I would like to go to Russia? If I don't like California, I sure as hell won't like Russia."

"Well, you're always so busy with your friends, I thought it would give us a chance to be alone for a while, and you could see some of the world. The company is picking up the tab."

The way she said "Let me think about it" wasn't promising.

The next night, she had his answer. "David, I'm not going to make the trip. You'll be working, and I'll just sit in some dingy hotel room all day."

"I'm sure there will be tours you can take." "No, I've made up my mind."

Ashley jumped into the conversation. "Mom, if you won't go, can I?" Her exuberance knew no bounds and was hard to subdue.

But Julia managed to do it. Turning slowly to her, Julia said, "How'd you get that idea?"

Ashley turned her appeal to David. "David, can I?"

David took a neutral stance. "This is something between you and your mother." Now in a more submissive tone, the young woman pleaded, "Mom, can I?" Julia walked off. Over her shoulder, she said, "Let me think about it."

Later, alone with Julia, David said, "I think the trip would be good for her." Julia said, "Let's sleep on it."

Julia was thinking, Hmm, it would. It can't be bad having Ash away and not snooping on me for a while. She's like a damn cop.

The next day, David got a call from Ashley. Her voice was upbeat. He could almost see the wry grin over the phone. "I can go! I can go! She didn't make any fuss over it at all. Ain't that cool?"

David smiled.

The Aeroflot Tupelov 124 with the Cyrillic lettering on its white side landed with a thump, a chirp of rubber, and the roar of reverse-thrusting engines. The pretty Russian flight escorts immediately began chanting deplaning instructions in English and Russian.

The Sheremetyevo airport wasn't a disappointment, seeming like a normal, bustling European airport. But the hotel, although one of the best, couldn't get past its sense of the medieval. Maybe it was the cracks on the gray outside walls and the lousy phone service, but Ashley was hopeful. After all, she was going to be alone with David.

In the men's room, the culture shock took multiple leaps. There was one dirty sink and one smelly urinal. The hinges on the door to the lone toilet stool was broken. The toilet set was broken off and leaning against the wall. You had to set the seat on top of the toilet stool and hope your movement didn't cause you to fall into the toilet. So this is the real Russia?

The next day, David was out on the job, being shown around the site by five eager young men. The nearest Russian said, "Have you seen anything yet that your company might be interested in?"

David hesitated. "You understand that our company is not a drilling company. We have a very extensive line of equipment and repair parts. I think we will be able to do business with any company that takes on this project."

Another Russian, a small man with a beard and goatee, piped in. "To give you a better understanding of the Russian way of life, I've made arrangements for a guide for you tomorrow. She'll take you around. When you're done, the three of us will meet back here."

David wondered about the strategy involved but had enough respect for international business practices to give them their head on the matter.

That afternoon, David found himself in a grocery store. He and his female guide were standing aside. She grabbed a jar of coffee off the shelf and handed it to him. "See that price?"

He said, "Uhhh, if my Russian is any good, I'd say it's three dollars and fifty cents."

"Correct. Now consider that our retired persons only get five dollars per month."

David made the appropriate surprised gestures. "Yep." People in the store erupted in bawdy laughter.

In the next store, which was a department store, a long line of people waiting to get in confronted David and his guide.

The guide, an attractive young woman with natural blond hair, said, "See all these people waiting? When the store opens, there won't be much to buy. Most of the goods are reserved at the commissary." She lowered her voice, "You know, for the leaders."

David said, "Yep."

Those customers within ear range burst out laughing.

A befuddled David shrugged it off. Back at the oil company offices, the guide was saying her farewells. A company exec interjected, "I'm glad to see the tour was educational."

With a big smile, the guide said, "Just one more thing before I go. Yep is Russian slang for wanting to have sex. The laughing was because they saw you as the horny American."

David reddened. "You mean I've been going all over Russia asking everyone if they want to f—?"

The girl, in an aside, said, "You mentioned how downtrodden the people looked. Well, they have very little joy in their lives. You gave them something to laugh about. It was a real pick-me-up."

David shook his head. "So be it."

That night, on his way up to his room in the elevator, he stood beside a gorgeous Russian woman. She asked, "Going up?"

He unconsciously said, "Yep." When he saw her flabbergasted yet amused reaction, he began to flounder. "I mean, no yep. No yep."

The woman, veiling her smile, just chuckled as he gladly exited the elevator at his stop.

David was sitting propped up on the bed, shuffling papers.

He found Ashley fresh from the shower, wrapped in a towel. She asked, "Can I keep you company while I read on the bed?"

Ashley plopped down on the bed, feet on the pillow, her head at the foot of the bed.

"Sure, just scoot over to the other side."

After she stretched out, he asked, "What are you reading?" "It's boring. For my biology class."

"It must be interesting. You seem so deeply engrossed in it. I thought it surely must be a chick novel."

"I'm reading how the various nerve endings affect emotions. It starts with the toes and works up."

David said "I'll just have to see if your book knows what it's talking about" as he reached down and began to nibble on her toes. At first, his thought was to just kid around, but he found himself quickly getting aroused by the beautiful and nubile young woman. Watching her squirm in pleasure was a huge turn-on.

"Hmmm, that feels so good," she murmured as she put the book down and rested her head on her folded arms. "Is this still part of the biology lesson, or are you going to make love to me?"

David began massaging her calves and working his way up to her thighs. She squirmed with pleasure. He kissed the back of her knee and smiled as it quivered. He said, "You okay? I'm not going too fast? You are a virgin, aren't you?" When she didn't answer, he asked again, "Aren't you?"

She nodded.

He slid his hands farther up her legs and inserted a finger into her wet womanhood and delighted in her sigh of delight.

Her voice muffled in her arms, Ashley muttered, "I know what's happening." "Want me to stop?"

"Hell, no." She rolled over on her back, raised her legs up to a bent-knee position, and reached for him.

The first kiss left them gasping; the second, longer, left them panting. A frantic, almost hysterical coupling put them into a world of surreality, of fantasy, of dreams. When they parted, both were sweaty and panting. Ashley murmured, "Wow, I can't believe it. Of all places to have my first climax—a mind-bending climax—it has to be in this dingy Russian hotel room. What in the world could be less sexy, less romantic, less erotic than a dingy Russian hotel room? But I'll never think of Russia in the same way. You were so wonderful I didn't need a romantic setting."

They were quiet for a while. Ashley said, "What are you thinking? Regrets?" "Maybe, but mostly I was wondering."

"What?"

"Why you're mother agreed for you to come on this trip? Do you think that maybe she wanted you to broaden your cultural horizons?"

Ashley gave a quick no.

"Why then would she send me off on a trip with a beautiful young woman who is not of my blood?"

"You really think I'm beautiful?"

David rolled his eyes. "Yeah, like you don't know it."

She turned coquettish. "Maybe, but a girl likes to know that her man thinks she's beautiful."

"I'm your man now?"

"Maybe you don't know it, but someday you will be. As for why Mom let me go with you, that's easy."

"Easy?" David looked at her blankly. "Maybe for you." "She wanted to get rid of me."

"Why?"

"So she could be with her dykey friends." "No."

"No what? That she didn't want to get rid of me or that she has dykey friends?" "Either."

"David, I love you, but you're a dork. Take it from a woman. No woman would send her husband off with a good-looking chick just because she's his stepdaughter and therefore not vulnerable."

Another quiet moment followed. Still naked, she rolled over to him. "Let's stop talking about her. I want you again."

Later, he said to her, "Any regrets?"

"Not a one. Only that I didn't read this book sooner. I want this feeling to go on forever. Promise me this won't be our last."

He thought about it. "Here I am, lecturing to you that we shouldn't be doing this, and you're making me promise that this is just the beginning. I'm only human, Ash. Give me a break. I want to be a good husband."

"How could you be a good husband when she doesn't give you any?" "How could you possibly know that?"

"I know the look of a contented man." He grinned. "How?"

"A woman knows."

"I can't think of you as a woman. I used to change your diapers." "Just tell me this is not our last time."

He thought for a moment. "Promise."

Ashley giggled. "Gee," she said, lapsing serious. "This makes life worth living."

David too seemed to be serious. "Funny thing about it is, I don't feel the least bit guilty about it."

"Why should you? Mom doesn't seem to care a hoot about either of us."

"It's not your place, Ashley, to get into Julia and my relationship. As far as you're concerned, or should be concerned, we are still married." David didn't really understand why he was adamant about that. She was still his daughter, stepdaughter or not, and he felt duty-bound to lecture her. What a hypocrite, he admonished himself.

In a petulant tone, Ashley said, "Does this mean that we won't be having sex again?"

"Not here in Russia. We leave in the morning."

"That means we have all night, and I think morning sex with you will be sensational."

"So what memories of Russia will you have other than sex?"

"Seventy-cent Big Macs. For a buck, you can have a whole meal. Can you believe that? I can't wait to tell my college friends. And that McDonald's must be the biggest in the world. I took pictures of McDonald's and the menu boards."

Just then there was a knock at the door. David was handed a courier message. Ashley said, "What is it?"

"The Russian plane has been taken out of service. We've been changed to SAS with a one-night layover in Helsinki. Ash, you sure called that one. Morning sex is off the charts."

It was a very early flight, which went smoothly, but when they arrived at the hotel, as usual, the room wasn't ready. The clerk pointed to the tourist office and suggested that they do some quick sightseeing.

It turned out to be fun. They toured the big underground Lutheran rock church and the park where Gorky Park was filmed because the Russians would not let the movie company into their country.

Back at the hotel, they paid a visit to the Finnish version of McDonald's. Ashley's eyes popped. "A Big Mac is eight dollars?"

"The fish fillet is seven US."

Back at the hotel, the room was ready. After getting settled, Ash said, "David, I'm going back to the hotel convenience store. I might find something for us to remember Helsinki."

While David was browsing the hotel lobby, waiting for Ash to come back, he was approached by a drop-dead gorgeous woman. "Are you interested in some company?" she asked.

"What do you charge?"

"Three hundred US for one hour."

"Can I have a free sample?" he kidded.

She didn't think that was funny. Miffed, her face stiffened. "You Americans! You want everything given to you," she snarled and stomped off.

The international flight was progressing uneventfully. David and Ashley snuggled, warm with the memories of their nights together.

A flight attendant was proceeding down the aisle, taking dinner orders. "Fish or reindeer?"

David did a double take. In a loud voice, he said, "I'll have a chunk of Bambi." Suddenly, two kids who overheard the conversation burst out crying. "He's going to eat Bambi."

It took some cajoling to convince the kids that David was only kidding. He wasn't going to eat Bambi.

CHAPTER THIRTEEN

Back home, Julia was in her living room, surrounded by most of her usual group. She was whining. "Oh, that damned annual fishing trip! I'll be stuck with David for a whole week. Do any of you know what it's like to be stuck in some flea- bitten cabin in the woods full of mosquitoes and bugs? And every day it's the same thing. Fishing. We can't set the tournament date until I find out when I have to go fishing. At least we've agreed on the rules and format."

That seemed to end the meeting, and everyone except Beth left in a flurry of air kisses and hugs.

Beth was tipsy. And she was aggressive. "Julia, I need to know. Do we have a future together? Or is it going to be all this sneaking around if and when it is convenient for you and your husband?"

As usual, Julia seemed to want to chair the question, but Beth pressed on. "But I don't want to invest any more of my time on our relationship. I don't feel comfortable being intimate with a bisexual. You don't know what he may bring home from his travels, if you know what I mean. I have to protect myself."

"Beth, I know you're right and I'm putting things off. I know it isn't fair to you, but if you will be a bit more patient... I'll be going on this fishing trip. I'll give some time to thinking about it. But I have to be honest. I have no way to support myself, especially with Ash in college. If you don't want to just be satisfied with what we have, I won't blame you for moving on. But," she said, lapsing sad, "I would miss you."

Both women became silent and contemplative.

"I don't want to, Beth. I truly care for you, and the sex is wonderful, but I have to live."

Julia leaned over, held the back of Beth's neck, and their lips sought each other. They kissed passionately, Julia's tongue probing. Beth breathlessly asked, "Do we have time now?"

Julia shook her head. "Sorry, babe, he'll be home any minute now."

Beth, now a little sloppily drunk and getting melancholy, hugged Julia. "You'll always be everything to me, no matter what you decide."

A couple of days later, Hazel, John, David, Julia, and Ashley were crammed among a load of camping gear in John's station wagon. David was at the wheel, John beside him, and the girls in the back.

They didn't round the first corner of their street when Hazel muttered, "I feel like I forgot something. The iron! I left it on! I know I did. The house is going to burn down, and it will be all my fault."

Everyone in the car chorused, "The iron is off!"

Ashley turned around, grabbed the iron, and held it up. "Look, Grandma, it can't be on." Everyone laughed, and the joke was on Hazel.

David occasionally glanced at Hazel and Ashley in the backseat. Ashley was sitting right behind him, and she manipulated her toes to wriggle under his butt.

David commented, "Itchy toes, Ash?" "Just needed to stretch my legs."

John piped in, "Hope the weather holds up. Rained most of the time last year." Ashley intoned, "I hope there are people my age around this time."

David, his tongue in his cheek mentally, said, "Maybe you'll find a little extra excitement this trip."

In the rearview mirror, David exchanged knowing glances with both Ashley and Hazel, Hazel offering a subtle wink.

As for David, the pressure was almost too great. Riding in a car for six hours with three women he was having sex with was proving too much for his libido.

The drive droned on, the hum of the tires on the road mesmerizing, the passing farmland no different than the last several miles.

John's conversation too never changed tone or pitch. "I like the big lake. Too much trouble getting a boat over that sandbar into the little one. Besides, there's more fish in the big lake."

A bit restless, David asked, "John, do you mind driving for a while? I'm fading fast. Julia, do you mind if I sit in the back? Easier on my back and I only need some time off from driving."

David pulled off the road. Julia joined her dad in the front seat, leaving David sitting between Hazel and Ashley.

While Julia was dozing, Hazel took David's hand and placed it on the seat beside her. She rolled her body slightly toward the window. David slipped his hand under her, covering it with his jacket. David asked John, "Do you know if the fishing rules have changed?"

"No, don't know. We'll get this year's rules when we get the fishing licenses." Hazel was squirming, her face getting flushed.

Julia awakened and looked around. "Dad, look at the fields of sunflowers. Remember when we had to walk the corn and bean fields, chopping them down?"

"Yeah, now it's a cash crop. I hated it when we lost the farm and moved to the city, but life, I have to admit, is much better now. There's something to be said about working for a paycheck rather than working the farm where you have to sweat everything from the weather to locusts."

Hazel turned her head toward the window, trying to conceal her excitement. Unable to resist, she climaxed, and a shudder shook her body. It got Ashley's attention, and she asked, "Are you all right, Grandma?"

Hazel said, "Oh sure, just a little chilly."

David manipulated his fingers, and Hazel, trying hard to keep it off her face, squirmed and moaned inwardly.

When Ashley said "David, would you put your jacket over me? It's cold," the game was up. But now he was able to caress Ashley's breasts.

John commented, "Not too much farther now, I reckon."

David said, "I hope you're right. I'm getting stiff." Ashley grinned. Hazel poked him in the ribs.

Finally, they pulled into the fishing camp at South Lake, Lida in Minnesota. Everyone got out and started to stretch before they began unloading. A large lake glistened through the trees, and in the distance was a smaller one connected by a sandbar. Cabins dotted the shoreline. Many were updated and upscale, but the one they rented was very plain and original, with few amenities. By now, Julia had become accustomed to much more luxurious accommodations, but her parents were conservative and rooted to all their old habits and thus the same lake, the same cabin for years.

Everyone was busy preparing the cabin for their stay. John said, "I'll go down to the docks and see if the boats we reserved are ready. Sometimes they get behind and can delay our start."

Julia said, "Ashley, you can help get things put away, okay? If I know Dad, he'll be down at the docks fussing around all day, gossiping about the fishing. David, would you take Mom to town for some groceries?"

David and Hazel exchanged naughty grins.

In the car, on the way to town, Hazel said, "You know, you made me come in the car."

"Good!"

"Yes, good, but not good enough. Now I'm frustrated for more."

"Well, if we hurry, we have enough time for a quickie on our way back. Tear the list in half so we can get done quicker." They hurried through the aisles of the store.

The checkout clerk asked them, "What's the hurry, folks?" David said, "Got to get back to the fishing."

The clerk said in a laconic upstate tone, "You don't have to worry. I'm pretty sure the fish will still be there."

Ignoring the clueless clerk, the couple checked out and hurried to the car. Halfway back to the cabin, they found a secluded spot off the narrow country road, parked, and scrambled into the backseat. They turned to each other, and David had Hazel's bra off in a matter of seconds as their passion consumed them. When they were satiated, Hazel giggled. "In all my years, I've never done it in the backseat of a car. I've heard so much about the backseats of cars, but this is a first."

David buckled his pants. "A good first?" She sighed. "The best."

When they got back to the cabin, nobody was around. David said, "They must be out, trying the boats."

"Great. That gives me time for a shower. I don't want any of you in me when they get back."

David casually watched as she got undressed. He said, "I think I'm up for another quickie before you jump in the shower. How about you? Is that gonna work?"

"Get in here, then. I'll have to take care of whatever you've got."

David rushed into the bedroom, undressing as he went. Hazel grabbed a hand mirror and smacked his cock, sending him howling.

After her shower, Hazel found him lying on the couch in her room. She turned her back to David and bent over to dry her legs.

David, chuckling, said, "Now that gives the golden arches a whole new meaning."

Hazel said, "Now let me see your owie. Let mommy kiss it and make it all better."

"Don't touch it. That thing's loaded. If it goes off, it'll blow your hand off and cause serious damage."

"I don't intend to touch it," she said, lowering her mouth to him. "I think I need the mirror again."

They were both half-undressed and giggling when they heard the drone of a motorboat approaching.

Hazel said, "OH Shit!'

She ran to the bathroom, and David headed for the living room on the run, trying to adjust his clothes.

A few minutes later, Julia, Ashley, and John came in. John said, "Well, the boats run real well. They tuned them up this year. They're ready for fishing." Ashley simply looked bored, as did Julia.

Julia said, "Dad, you and Mom have the large bedroom. David and I have the small bedroom, and Ashley—"

The young girl moaned, "I know, I get the couch as always."

John grabbed a water glass and, holding it up, said, "Everyone put ten dollars in it. First catch gets the money."

After dinner, John announced, "Okay, everybody, off to bed. Fishing early tomorrow. You know we have to get up and out of here before the sun comes up." Julia and Ashley looked less than thrilled.

In the morning, they had a light breakfast of coffee, toast, and pastry and headed for the lake. It was a clear Northwoods morning. The lake was flat calm. Only high-flying cumulus clouds were in sight. The water was sparkling, its blue startling against the green evergreen woods. John and Hazel loaded their gear into one boat, and the rest got in the other.

After an hour of fishing, Ashley was just about asleep when she was awakened by a tug on her line. Eventually, she pulled in a small perch. "I win! First fish of the trip wins!"

Julia called out, "Doesn't count. That's not a keeper. The rules say it has to be at least a pound."

From the next boat, John called out, "Does too count. No rule says it has to be a keeper. Ashley wins. She gets ten bucks from everybody." He was already having a great time.

The next morning, they were finishing breakfast, taking the last sips of coffee. John said, "Fishing is slow. I hope it picks up. No fun sitting there watching the lake and dozing off."

Hazel said, "John, I'm up for a walk. Anybody want to tag along?" Ashley volunteered.

Julia said, "As for me, I'm going to finish the night's sleep. Damned mosquitoes kept me up last night."

"Sure," said David, "you three go ahead."

After everyone departed, David went into their bedroom and lay down on the bed next to Julia. There were times in his life when David craved a normal husband-and-wife relationship and a normal love life. Sometimes the three-ring circus he was running was not only exhausting but it also heightened his sense of paranoia and of getting caught.

He spooned his body to Julia's, only to get the usual shrug and complaint. There was only one thing that worked, and he had to be careful about it. After he began rubbing her back and then started caressing her breasts, he would quickly slip down between her legs and perform oral sex. He had to do it slowly and with great finesse and while she was still half-asleep. After she was panting with desire, he mounted her and finished in the normal way. The things she muttered and mumbled half-asleep made it seem that she didn't even realize whom she was making love to. If he didn't use this technique, he would find himself making love to a zombie. She didn't move a muscle, clearly not into it. Or she'd whine, "David, I'm trying to rest. Didn't I tell you I didn't sleep well last night? I'm in no mood for sex, if that's what you're thinking."

His answers would range from "We hadn't had sex in a long time" or "We won't have many chances to be alone. I just thought…" "Just go away and leave me alone."

Today it didn't work. Miffed, not only at the turndown but also at the attitude, he grabbed his briefcase, went out onto the deck, and began perusing papers. Suddenly, Ashley crept up on him from behind and caught him by surprise. She said, "Let's go somewhere we can be alone. I just want to be near you with no one else around."

He was more than eager and readily agreed. "Okay, that island out there is pretty secluded. Let's head out that way."

Bringing their fishing gear for cover, the two set out for the island. As they neared the island near the shore, there was a marsh, and David used an oar to push the boat through the tall weeds to firm ground.

Ashley, in her youthful enthusiasm, called out, "Let's make this our island." "Like Bali Hai?"

"No, Bali Hai is too mystical, too corny. No such place. I was thinking more like Dolly and Kenny's 'Islands in the Stream.' Doesn't that describe our relationship? I feel each time we're together is an island of time, and we jump from island to island, taking our pleasure where and when we can. How many more islands are there for us?"

David intoned, "Someday, Mr. Right will come along and off you'll go."

"I don't want to think about it. All I really want is you. You do know that, don't you? If you don't, it's time that you stop thinking of me as a little girl."

"You are a little girl, Ash, at least compared to me. That's why I keep trying to discourage this wild idea you have about us having a future together. Think about it—when I'm sixty and going to the bathroom five times a night, you'll still be in your prime. You won't be happy with an old man."

Her bottom lip quivered. "David, don't say that. I want to be with you forever, for the rest of our lives. Don't talk like that. Sometimes my dream about a life with you is the only thing that keeps me going.

"I hate when you talk like that. I'm happiest when I see the future my way, and that's you and me together, for life. You know I'm right! I see Mom with all her dykey friends—what interest could she have in you?"

Even though he knew she was right, he refused to believe what a mess his life was. Let's face it, having three women in your life, all related, could get extremely complicated, and sometimes he got really sick of the lies.

Ashley was droning on. "Who are you more happy with, Mom or me? What interest does she have in you other than what—" In exasperation, she stopped. "I don't want to talk about it now. Let's explore our island."

David threw the anchor in to shore and turned to her, holding out his arms. In an effort to get away from the serious conversation that was developing, he took on a pseudo-gallant role and proclaimed, "Allow me, my lady." David picked up Ashley and set her on shore.

Feigning a Sir Francis Raleigh pose, he bowed low and said, "I claim this island in the name of Lady Ashley. Be it proclaimed throughout the realm, henceforth this will be known as Ashley's Island." Sometimes role-playing and making it all a big joke were the only ways he could get through it.

Ashley, getting into the mood, and in her own feigned British accent, said, "Let the noble conqueror be rewarded with a special favor. Let's be off to explore the virgin territory. If there are any virgins here, let your presence be known."

David quipped, "If we find any, can I have one?"

Ashley slapped his arm. "Behave, sir knight, or be beheaded."

"Beheaded?" he said. "Which head, the big one or the small one? I think I can use one more than the other in the afterlife."

She rolled her eyes, took his hand, and strolled off into the woods. In a shady and secluded glen, Ashley pulled David to the ground and sat on top of him.

He exclaimed. "Stop! I can't breathe. And besides, I can't make love with my boots on."

She was naked in a flash and straddled him. Later, lying together completely satiated and drying off with cool sweat, Ashley said, "I'm going down to the water to wash up. I don't want any of you on me when we get back."

"You know, if I was a more sensitive guy, I could take offense at that. How come I don't want to wash you off me?" She looked at him as if she were contemplating answering him and then headed to the lake.

Just like her grandmother.

A couple of days later, David and John were cleaning fish. Ashley came in with a note. "Here, David, this was hanging on the door when we got back to the cabin."

David said, "Lay it out of the way. I'll read it after we're done."

"I'll take these up to the office," John said, "to freeze with the rest of our catch."

David washed and dried his hands and then picked up the note. It read, "Call me ASAP. Austy."

Though not the paranoid type, David still had an uneasy feeling about whatever it was about. He called the office and got the CEO's assistant, asking, "Jennifer, what's up? I got this message to call the boss."

She sounded hesitant. Then she said, "David, you know he wouldn't tell me a thing like that. Besides, I'm a confidential secretary—if I told you, I'd be out of a job. I'll put you through to Mr. Houser."

That fueled what little paranoia was still lurking.

Austy Houser came on the line. "Sorry, David, I'm going to have to ask you to cut your trip short. No, I can't tell you over the phone. The company plane will be at the airport at two o'clock tomorrow. No, you'll be coming back to the office."

Everyone was sitting in the cabin living room when David came in, looking concerned. He told them, "Sorry, guys, looks like I'm going to have to cut my vacation a bit short this time." Hazel and Ashley exchanged concerned looks.

Hazel asked, "Why, David? What's wrong?"

"Not sure exactly. But something is going on at the office. My boss wants me back tomorrow. I leave tomorrow afternoon."

Ashley intervened, "Can I go back with you? Really, it's so boring here with nobody my own age."

Julia said, "All right with me, Ash. I understand not being around the people you want to."

Ashley flew upstairs to pack.

Hazel turned to David. "Want to take me fishing tomorrow one more time before you go?"

"Absolutely."

In the morning, under a clear sky, David piloted the skiff up to the sandbar that adjoined the big lake to the little lake. David and Hazel hopped out and began to pull the skiff over the sandbar and into the little lake. Hazel said, "Head for my tree. It's deep in the woods and completely out of sight."

David steered the boat to a big Douglas fir on the far shore, the one she referred to as her tree.

They stood facing each other. David said, "I don't want this to be a quickie. We don't know when we'll be together again." So he slowly undressed her as she did him. They stood caressing each other and deeply kissing till they couldn't stand it anymore and sank to the ground onto a blanket they had brought. Their embrace was tight and almost desperate. They did all their familiar positions till both were exhausted. He jokingly said to her, "I'm waiting for the day when I wear you out first, when I leave you worn out while I'm still ready to go."

"That day might not come. I'll always want to keep up with you."

On the way back, Hazel whimsically said, "I love you, my little lake"—and she turned to look back—"and my big tree."

"Yeah, fishing was always good here," he quipped with a smarmy grin. She slapped his arm.

Hazel said, "You never have to fish, the fish come to you. I'm going down to the water for a bath."

"I know," he said, "you don't want me on you."

When David and Hazel got back to the cabin from their sexcapade, David had to shower, get dressed, and pack. Addressing Julia, John, and Hazel, he said, "Are you sure you can get back okay?"

John said, "We've made this trip many times before you came along, my boy." Ashley, pacing the floor, admonished, "Hurry up, David, let's get going." David said, "We're lucky there's an airport nearby we can use."

CHAPTER FOURTEEN

At noon, John drove David and Ashley to the local airport, and they boarded the company aircraft, a Hawker 4000. The pilot, Doug, was doing his preflight check. Doug was a good-looking guy and had the flair of the pilot, confident to the point of cockiness and outgoing. David asked, "Got room for a hitchhiker?"

Doug eyed Ashley. "For her? Sure do."

David made the introductions. "This is my stepdaughter, Ashley. She's never been in a private plane."

Doug grinned. "I'll do my best to impress her, Mr. March. It isn't often I get such pretty passengers."

She began to explore the aircraft, calling from the back. "Hey, David, there's a bed back here."

"Yep," David said, "it comes in handy on long trips, when you have to be fresh when you arrive at your destination. You know, especially if you're meeting female clients, you don't want to be smelly and sweaty."

She quipped, "Oh, I see, one needs to be fresh."

Doug said, "Yeah, I go back there for a snooze all the time." Ashley emerged, bug-eyed, her jaw tight. "Who flies the plane?"

Both men broke out in laughter. "Got you," Doug said, still chuckling at her innocence. A couple of hours later, after a bit of a bumpy flight in which Ashley clung to David's arm, they were on the final approach to Omaha International.

During the flight, Doug did his best to impress Ashley by explaining all the controls to her. He let her listen in on the right-hand seat radio to all the commands and weather reports. She was duly impressed. She knew when a guy was interested in her. He even let her sit in the left-hand seat and put her hand on the yoke and, for a very brief period of time, actually fly the aircraft. David smiled at Doug's antics like a benevolent father. She was thrilled to have a front-row seat to the landing. She was fascinated. First the long black runway in the distance, then breaking through the low cloud cover, then the voice from the control tower advising them it was clear to land, Then the landing.

Later on, David was lying on his bed at home. Ashley called out from the doorway, "Are you decent?"

He said, "No."

"Good, keep it that way." She entered, completely nude, carrying a tray with champagne and two glasses. Her body was firm and taut, tanned all over, even her big round breasts. She said, "Coffee, tea, or me?"

"Man!" he exclaimed, "I never had nipples with my champagne before." In a coquettish mood, she cooed, "Which do you want first?"

David made a great spectacle of trying to decide. "If I choose champagne, the nipples will get cold. If I choose nipples, the champagne will get warm." He shook his head in great consternation. "Oh, what to do, what to do?" He paused, thinking, while she feigned boredom. "Okay," he said, "I got it. I've made up my mind. It's not practical to get champagne cold again, but getting nipples warm is easy. A few minutes in my mouth and they're warm again. Okay, I've decided. Let's drink the champagne first." Ashley made a great display of pouring the champagne and serving it.

Ashley crawled under the covers, and they lifted their glasses. "To fishing," she announced.

"Not," he answered.

In the morning, David was in Austy's office. David said, "Well, I hope you didn't call me in to pick up my final check."

"Oh no, but I'll cut to the chase. The board is about to meet about buying out Unidraulics. You knew or heard the rumors that Ed Rolf has been wanting to sell the company, didn't you?"

"Oh yeah. Poor guy lost his wife too soon. He was so attached to her. His good- for-nothing kids never even visit him. What a lousy way to end up. Bust your hump all your life and wind up alone."

Austy sat back and leveled his gaze at David. "Well, David, we're interested. If the board approves the buyout, I want you to head the operation. Of course, it means moving to San Francisco and everything that goes with it—selling the old house, finding a new house, and adjusting to a new social circle. I know your wife has a lot of good friends here and would hate to lose them and that it might be a problem for you, but, my boy, an opportunity like this comes along only once in a lifetime.

David, who couldn't agree more, simply said "I know." But, his face brightening, he faced Mark and said, "Big challenge, great opportunity—I'm in. You're right, I'll be able to run the company my own way from the very beginning, and from what I hear, it's already a going concern."

Sitting up straight and extending his hand, Austy said, "Well, that's great news, David." He glanced at his wristwatch and said, "The board should just about be finishing up with the vote. Let's join them."

The board was indeed just about finishing up on the vote. One member said, "Well, Austy and David, we just voted to buy Unidraulics. But frankly, it all still keys on David. He knows the equipment better than anybody, and it will be up to him to make sure we are getting a good deal. So providing David agrees to go out there and assess the state of the company for a few days and takes a look around, sees if there are any rats hiding in the closet, then we'll decide based on his assessment."

David said, "I'll leave tomorrow."

He immediately got on the phone to Julia. "Well, there are some big changes in store for us. It looks like I will be heading the company's new acquisition in San Francisco. I have to check out the plant first for a few days, and I am going to bring Ashley along if that's all right with you, okay?" It always amazed him how Julia never or rarely objected to him taking his beautiful stepdaughter along with him on his trips. Some women might not be so compliant about something like that. After all, Ashey was a beautiful girl and he was a virile man, and they weren't related by blood.

"Good, I'll let her know to get her stuff together, bye."

Boy, he thought, that was pretty blunt and perfunctory. I would think she'd raise hell about leaving her friends. His mind was made up, and he was going to do it regardless of Julia. At this point, they pretty much led separate lives anyway. After the time at the cabin, he was pretty sure she had no use for him. That, along with the lady friends and the constant events, he began to wonder.

As soon as the call was over Julia sought out her mother, a petulant look on her face. Wearing her almost perpetual frown, Julia whined to her mother. "I can't believe it. David wants me to move back to California. He got a promotion and has to move. He knows I hate California. I hate everything about it. As far as I'm concerned, it's the land of fruits and nuts. Besides, my friends are all here."

Hazel's hand absently went to her throat. "Oh dear, it can't be that bad. I've always heard what a beautiful place California is. You won't have the dreadful winters we have to put up with in Nebraska."

Julia, in a full-fledged hissy fit, snapped, "No, I'd rather have the winters than all that phony California crap. It's not going to happen. David is going to have to go alone until we can figure something else out. No"—she stamped her foot like a whiny child—"it's not going to happen. It won't because I'm not going. David will just have to commute or use the corporate jet if he wants to see me." Hazel could see that she was dead serious and was not about to try to argue with her.

"That just isn't right, Julia. A woman belongs with her husband. You're getting a bit long in the tooth for a long-distance relationship, don't you think? I would think that you would know that."

"No, what's not right is his moving me to a place I hate. He's the one who should have more consideration for me."

"But, darling, it isn't like he has a choice. If that is required of him, he is doing it not only for himself but also for his family. He is in the type of business that he has to go where the business is. It's not like he is an accountant or has some job that keeps him rooted to his desk and in one place."

The comment simply didn't register with Julia. Hazel might as well not have said it. Hazel rarely got distraught, but she was now. "You played house with that first guy, and it didn't get you anywhere. To save face, you quit your job and married the first guy that came along. Now you're talking about living apart from David. It's just not right. A wife should pick up and go with her husband."

With a toss of her head, Julia said, "I don't care, Mom."

On the way to the airport, in the company limousine, David and Ashley were marveling at the accommodations the company were providing—a penthouse right downtown! "How much did you say it was worth again?" she asked.

"Well, considering where it's located and all the amenities it has, I'd say a good two million at least, maybe more when you count all the security systems and crazy electronics Ed installed. He's made it into a dream house. It's been a kind of hobby of his while his wife was alive. He always wanted to surprise her with the latest cutting-edge gadgets."

Ashley said, "What a lovely man."

At the airport, they met the pilot, Doug, and boarded the plane. Doug took an extra-long peek at Ashley's legs as she seated herself on the lounge chair. She was cooing. "I can't believe this is really happening. I keep thinking I'm gonna wake up and we're really staying at some mom-and-pop motel or, even worse," she said giggling, "the cabin at the lake."

Later that day, they were ensconced in the incredibly impressive penthouse with every modern convenience known. It was high on Russian Hill, with a panoramic view of San Francisco, the bridge, and the bay. It had an indoor Jacuzzi, three baths, electronically operated drapes, a wet bar, and a fully applianced stainless- steel kitchen. In the living room was an entertainment center that was cutting-edge, with a huge wall TV and a surround-sound hi-fi system. The security system on the wall by the door was cutting-edge with a key card-entry system. David was sitting at the massive dining room table, going over paperwork, while Ashley walked into the room, looking very sexy in a short black dress with red high heels. "I'm so glad," he said, "that Doug asked to show you the town."

She pouted. "Already you're pawning me off to another man."

"Yeah, that's the way it should be. Well, you should be with people your own age, especially a dashing young pilot type."

Ashley frowned. "When you talk like that, it sounds to me like you're trying to get rid of me."

"I would never do that," he quipped. "Do you think you can remember how to use the elevator eye card and code? This place is like a damned fortress."

"Yeah. If not, I'll just call your cell. Hey, how do I look?" "Great. In your pilot dress."

"Pilot dress?"

"Yeah, it ends just below the cockpit."

She had to think about it. She muttered, thinking, "Below the cockpit? The cockpit?" Then she brightened. "Oh, I get it. You dirty old man! And your pilot better not be a dirty young man."

Ashley laughed and, with her left hand, reached down, grabbing the hem of her dress and pulling it up to the side of her sleek long leg, exposing her black panties. She gave her hip a couple of shakes in David's direction, sticking out her tongue. "I'm sure Doug is going to love my outfit."

"I'm sure too."

The intercom buzzed. She rushed to answer the intercom buzzer. "Hello? Doug?"

"Yeah, it's me. How do I get up there?"

She giggled. "It's too complicated. I'll be right down." She clicked off the intercom.

David said, "Have a great time. It's your town, babe. But try to keep Doug's sightseeing confined to the tourist sites."

The ringing phone interrupted David's newspaper reading.

It was Ashley. "David, did you remember to call the rental car company?" "How's your evening going?"

Ashley said, "I'm freezing my ass off. Doug had this parka. It doesn't do anything for my figure, but it's warm." She added for a second time, "Hey, did you remember to call the car rental company?"

"It's all taken care of."

The girl beamed. "Just being a good wife. I didn't want you to be late for work on your first day. You know, David, it's pretty cold out here. I'll be wanting to feel something warm over me when I get back, and I don't mean any blanket or parka. Get my drift? No blanket, no parka."

"I got it. I'll see what I can do."

David was reading paperwork in bed when she slipped in. "Ash, how was your evening?"

"Fun but cold until the end. Men! Yuck! He took me to all the romantic places like the Top of the Mark, the cable cars, Chinatown, and then he puts the moves on. Sheesh. Whatever happened to dating a girl awhile? Everybody wants to get laid on the first date. There's no romance. It's a few drinks and into the sack."

"You're just an old-fashioned girl, Ash, even though you don't know it. Most girls raised in Nebraska are like that."

"I am?"

"Well, you're not doing the modern cool-girl stuff. You know, the Girls Gone Wild stuff—flashing their boobs every chance they get, doing Jell-O shots off bellies on the top of a bar, and getting loaded and using that as an excuse to go to bed with the first guy who takes them home."

She had to think about that for a while. "You know, you know me better than anybody. I'm really not cool with that stuff—bunch of chicks flashing everybody so as to be admired. All they get is a gang bang out of it and tell themselves it was hot. Hot, my butt! It's just degrading. They buy you a drink and they think you owe them a game of backseat bingo. Got room for one more in there?"

"Hop in."

Ashley curled up beside him, and they drifted off to sleep in each other's arms.

CHAPTER FIFTEEN

David knew that the best way to find out what was happening in any organization was to pop up unexpected. So he show up up at the guard shack at Unidraulics early.

The guard seemed to know he was coming. There was nothing out of place in his regulation uniform. Even his hat was set at the exact proper angle. "Good morning, Mr. March. We knew you'd be coming today, but we didn't expect you so early."

David said, "You knew my name. What's yours?" "I'm Al Parker. You can call me Al."

"I'm David. You can call me Dave or David."

The guard's facial expression changed so slightly only an observant person like David would ever notice, so he waited for some kind of response.

"Oh, that's very kind of you, sir. We're used to formality around here. That's going to take some getting used to."

David smiled to put the man at ease. "What sort of things do you check for here at the guard shack?"

Al was quick with his answers. "Well, sir"—David smiled at him— "uh, David, the first thing we check for are expired badges, fake badges, things like that."

"Why would ex-employees be trying to get back in?"

Al hesitated. "Never thought much about that, sir—uh, sorry— David. I don't know why. But whatever the reason, it can't be good."

David grinned. "You're right there, Al."

Motioning toward a nearby parking spot, he asked, "Is this where I'll be parking?"

"No, you'll be parking in the executive parking lot on the other side of the complex. You have to park here now 'cause of your rental car. Would you like me to have someone show you where it is later?"

"That'd be great, Al. Place is so big I might waste half a day finding it. I sure like the way you greet the oncoming shift, Al."

The guard beamed. "I'm the first person they see. I hope to give them a little lift."

"Do any of the management personnel come out here?"

"Heck, no. They're much too important. Most of them won't give me the time of day."

"I see," said David solemnly. "Well, anyway, I'm all for the way you handle your job."

Al beamed again, deeper this time. "Thank you, sir," he said, forgetting the formality issue again, but giving Dave a two-fingered salute to the brim of his cap.

Dave drove on in. Obviously, Al was on his best behavior, but there was something sincere about the man that David prided himself in spotting good people.

As soon as his car was parked, David headed for the building lobby. He walked in and took a look around. It was empty except for a lone receptionist at her desk. She appeared to be daydreaming as David approached her. "Hi, miss, I'm David March. I'm here to see…"

"Oh yes, Mr. March, let me buzz his assistant."

David took the liberty of wandering around the lobby and casually eavesdropping. From the overheard conversations, he heard a lot of gossiping, none of it having to do with the company's business.

Wandering back to the receptionist, he asked, "Where are all the managers?"

The receptionist was eager to answer, a sense of pride in being on top of things. "Oh, they're all in the conference room. They always start the day with a couple of hours of round-table discussions."

David's reaction was not what she might have expected, but in any case, he kept it to himself. Two hours of round table? Every day?

The staccato click-clack of high heels on the marble floor announced the assistant, a beautiful tall young woman with sleek long legs, approaching David with her hand extended.

"Good morning, Mr. March, I'm Grace. Let me show you to Mr. Rolf's office."

They made small talk on the way to Rolf's office. Ed Rolf, a robust sixty-eight- year-old, rose from his chair to greet David. "So we meet again. Did you ever think that someday you may be running the company?"

David smiled. "It's not a done deal yet. This is just a fact-finding expedition." Rolf flashed a smile. "Well, if it's any indication, your due-diligence team liked what they saw. All the department heads are in the conference room. It's your show now. Let 'em have it, David."

Grace then escorted David to the conference room.

About twenty executive types were sitting around the large mahogany conference table. Without exception, all eyes were on Grace and her equally beautiful assistant, Alice, before they all shifted to David.

David started with, "Good morning, gentlemen. My name is David March, and you all know why I'm here. The diligence reports look good. If I find things satisfactory, the purchase will proceed. To get to the root of your concerns, Grace and Alice will facilitate a transition workshop."

The girls exchanged puzzled glances.

David continued. "While I'm touring the company, Grace and Alice will list on butcher paper all your concerns and questions as to what the future may hold related to management. I will then assess your concerns and give them great thought. Let's go to work!"

Grace and Alice were standing quietly by as David was looking over copious notes that were taped to the walls.

David said, "Okay, kids, lots of good info here. Thanks for all your help."

As they were preparing to break up the meeting, Alice asked, "Mr. March, can Grace and I add a few items?"

David grinned. "Please call me David. Second, yeah, I need to hear all that concerns the company."

Grace said, "I've never heard of a transmission workshop. But this was the most productive meeting I've ever attended." Alice agreed with a head nod.

David said, "It's a transition workshop. However, we will be changing gears. I still have a couple of days here, but from what I've seen, if the sale goes through, this company is in for a big jolt." His head ratcheted from one girl to the other. He asked, "If you two knew things weren't right, why didn't you say something?"

Both exchanged a double take. Grace said, "That's a sure way to lose your job.

It's nice to be an idealist, but a girl has to pay her rent first. At this point, we can still lose our jobs."

"How so?"

"Well," said Alice, "we know that when companies change hands, the new owners usually want to bring in their own people. You know, people they know and trust."

David made sure he made eye contact with each woman. "Anyone who would replace competent, knowledgeable, and experienced people is a fool. And, ladies, I'm no fool."

Their smiles lit up the room.

CHAPTER SIXTEEN

Ashley and David were packing to leave San Francisco. David commented, "Well, Ash, ready to leave your city?"

Ashley's sigh was as whimsical as it was heartfelt. "This has been the best vacation of my life."

Snapping his briefcase shut, David said, "I'll be going out to the plant to tie up a couple of loose ends. I'll be back to get you for our one o'clock departure. I'll leave you to strip the beds."

"Why beds? We only used the master."

"Alice will be coming in with the cleaning crew. We need to cover our tracks as if we used two beds. Can't leave any incriminating DNA."

With a coquettish grin, Ashley said, "I'd better go upstairs and mess up my bathroom too."

Back over at Unidraulics, David was sitting behind a desk, and Grace was taking notes.

David said, "I'm pretty sure we will be buying the company."

Grace took a twist of her raven hair. "I feel so sad for Mr. Rolf. He's so lonely now." Her mind obviously drifted back. She said, "You should have seen him when Mrs. Rolf was still alive. They would slip out for high tea at the Saint Francis. When he returned, he'd be just like a little kid."

As he stood, David lowered his voice into a more confidential tone. "While I'm gone, I want you and Alice on the QT to plan a big farewell send-off for Ed. Make a list of all his business associates and other people you feel should be invited. Fax me the plan. I'll put the chop on it and tell you when to start the ball rolling."

"Sounds great! Our driver will follow you to turn in your rental and see you off. I hope to see you back here soon. It will be a pleasure working for you."

Grinning, David said, "Until I get my feet off the ground, it will be more like I'll be working for you."

Ashley wasn't a particularly pretentious young woman, but boarding a private corporate jet in an exclusive part of the airport would be enough to turn any young woman's head. She felt special and couldn't deny it. David grinned. "Feel like a big shot?"

She slammed his arm. "Noo, I'm not like—okay, yes!"

Doug was being very professional, no longer making flirtatious remarks. When he got the word from the tower, he announced over the intercom, "Ready for takeoff."

David and Ashley were sitting at opposite ends of the lounge, and he was engaging in what was becoming a bit of a fetish for them—he was massaging her feet. Suddenly, a twinkle in his eye, he said, "Wanna join the mile high club?"

"What kind of a club is that? What do you have to do?"

He grinned. "You have to make love over ten thousand feet." A smile played across Ashley's pretty face.

David said, "There's a bed in the back." "What about the crew?"

David smiled. "Let them get their own dates." He pushed the intercom and announced to the crew, "Hey, guys, we're all set back here for a while."

The crew knew that was a covert excuse and the equivalent of the Do Not Disturb sign.

Doug reported back, "Roger that."

In the bedroom, Ashley started to undress. She was down to her bra when David said, "I'd better lay my coat on the bed. DNA, ya know."

She unhooked her bra and giggled. "You've been watching too much Law and Order."

The lovemaking had a particular passion to it. Their rhythm began to equal the droning of the engines, and when they finished in a heart-stopping climax, the plane lurched a bit. Ashley giggled. "I think I just lost my heart."

Ashley, lurching a bit toward the private restroom, murmured, "I gotta freshen up. I look like I've just been ravished." Grinning, she said, "How'd you like the Rice-A-Roni present?"

David looked around the room, searching. "I don't see it. Did I miss it?"

Ashley, laughing, said, "You know, Rice-A-Roni, the oral San Francisco treat?" He laughed.

David said, "Don't use the towels! Can't leave any evidence." "What do I use?"

"Don't you have any 'manhole covers'?" "Manhole covers? What's that?"

David said, "The things you use when you have your period."

Back home, David was lying in bed, fighting off the after-sex lethargy. When he emerged from the shower, he confronted Ashley. "Hey, Ash, you look as pale as your name. What's up? Are you sick?"

"Oh, it's nothing that a few manhole covers won't fix. I guess no sex for a few days."

"Wait, haven't you heard of the 'three holes, two hands' game?" "Say what?"

Laughing, David said, "You have three holes and two hands—cover the two you don't want used."

Ashley rolled her eyes. "I never realized how sick you were." She threw a box of Kleenex at him.

David lapsed serious. "The fishing party comes home Sunday. We'll need to go to the grocery store and stock up the house. We'll plan something special in case your grandma and grandpa want to stay for dinner."

As the two walked the aisles of the local grocery store, Ashley announced, "I'm going over to the hardware department and pick up some manhole covers."

Two matronly ladies overheard Ashley and exchanged puzzled looks.

When Ashley returned with an armload of women's hygiene products, the two ladies craned their necks to see better and, when they did, hurried off, red-faced, down the aisle, muttering, "Well, I never."

Ashley commented, "I bet that's true."

CHAPTER SEVENTEEN

The family decided on Hazel's house for their annual fish fry. Julia led the way, happy to be back in her own element. She rang the front doorbell and called out, "Here we are, ready to eat fish."

Hazel's face was flushed from the heat of the kitchen-cooking activity. She said, "I hope you're hungry. John's in the kitchen, breading the fish, gettin' ready to put 'em in the pan. We can visit in the kitchen while we get the rest put together." She turned to Ashley, "Okay, Ashley, I want to hear all about San Francisco."

Julia let out an exaggerated gasp. "Not again. I've heard it over and over again—the city, my city. Screw the city. I didn't like California when we lived there. I didn't like San Francisco. The whole damn place sucks. It should be named Vacuum Cleaner."

Hazel chastised her daughter. "Now, Julia, don't talk like that. Go ahead, Ashley, tell me all about it."

Breathlessly, Ashley launched into her travelogue. "There's so much to tell. It's wonderful! The condo was grand, close to everything, great shopping. We were driving up this hill—David, what was the name of that street?"

"Lombard Street."

"Yeah, that's it. Just before we got to the top, David stopped and told me to drive. Well, when I got to the top and started down, there it was—the curviest street in the world. We went to this place called the Cliff House for breakfast. They have this Johnson's Omelet stuffed with crab, sour cream, avocado, and bean sprouts. We sipped champagne as we watched and listened to the seals barking out on Seal Rock. We went to this place called the Edinburgh Castle for dinner. We ate fish and chips that came wrapped in newspaper, and you sprinkle malt vinegar on. A bagpiper comes in all dressed up and plays. And the cable cars are fun to ride!"

Hazel turned to John and, shaking a large wooden spoon at him, said, "John, that is where our next vacation is going to be."

John, his face dour, said, "I haven't heard anything I'd give up fishing for, and if Julia doesn't want to go, I'll go by myself."

Hazel glared at him. "Have fun! I'm sure you'll enjoy your own company." Ashley said, "Mom, I'm sure once you get out there and find your way around, you'll change your mind."

Julia said, "I've decided to let David go out first and get settled in his new position before I go through moving again."

There was a glint of anger in David's eyes. "We haven't talked about any of this yet, and you've gone ahead and made up your mind."

Sulking a bit, she answered, "My life is getting peaceful and comfortable here. I like it the way it is."

CHAPTER EIGHTEEN

David and Austy were sitting in his office, chatting about business. Austy said, "David, we're buying Unidraulics. I'd like you out there as soon as you can."

"What about the condo?"

"That's Unidraulics property. It now belongs to us." David nodded. "It's a great place to live."

Austy said, "Can't wait to pay you a visit."

Ashley was sitting in the kitchen, at home at midmorning. Julia, having just awoken, entered the kitchen. She noticed her daughter 's depression. She momentarily ignored it. "David go to the office?"

"No."

"Where did he go, then?" "San Francisco."

"Bastard. He didn't even say good-bye."

"He did it to me too, but you weren't interested enough to get out of bed." Looking a bit perplexed, Julia raced to the garage. She called Ashley, her tone excited. "Look!" There in front of them was a BMW with a huge bow on the top.

The tag read, "Ashley, I hope this car gives you as much pleasure as it has me. David." Her face brightened up immediately. Julia looked only a bit more uninterested than usual.

David was meeting with Ed Rolf at the company. Rolf said, "David, that was a great farewell gathering. It's been years since I'd seen some of those people."

"Yeah, Grace and Alice sure know how to throw a party."

"Well, good luck once again. You know where to find me if you need me. My house in Marin County is just down the road."

"Don't wait for trouble to brew. Come and visit with us anytime. You know you're always welcome."

After Ed left, David pressed the intercom button for Grace and Alice. Once they're in the office, he said, "Sit down, I need to hear the full extent of your concerns. This may take some time. Can I get you some coffee?"

Grace looked aghast. "Get me coffee? Am I in the right place? The CEO offering to serve coffee?" They all had a good chuckle over that.

David lapsed serious. "You watch my back, and I'll watch yours. Let me have it with both barrels."

Grace started. "It's more Alice's problem. I'm just a sounding board. Okay, Alice, you're on. Don't hold anything back."

Alice crossed her legs in a whisper of silk, which momentarily distracted David. Then she started talking. "Mr. Rolf let things get pretty lax. He has allowed each department head to hire their own administrative staff. Because of this, my administrative staff has been cut. However, my workload has increased."

"Alice, go ahead. Tell it like it is."

Alice said, "They have emotional connections with the women they hired." David eye's dilated. "You mean the name should be Unidabrothel?"

Grace laughed. "Boy, you get the point quick."

"I didn't graduate intelligence come lotta. My PHD is a post-hole digger." Grace said, "Jennifer told me you didn't call a spade a spade."

David chuckled. "It's a fuckin' shovel!"

Grace said, "Yeah, that's what Jennifer said."

David said, "Alice, prepare a memo to all department heads. One, all admin work will be done in the admin office. Two, to bring Unidraulics into compliance with corporate, all present employees will be retained if they meet corporate hiring requirements. Three, the CEO will conduct the department heads', middle management's, and first level management's interviews. Four, first-level managers approved by the CEO will be authorized to interview production workers and refer them to personnel for final acceptance. Five, admin supervisor will conduct administrative employees' interviews by appointment. Six, personnel will be responsible for certifying all other employees. Grace, Alice, anything you want to add?"

When he was finished with the memo, the girls were slack-jawed. Alice said, "The revolving door around here is gonna seem like a tornado is moving it."

Now it was David's turn to look stunned. "Is it really that bad?"

Grace was grinning from ear to ear now. "You're going to need a backhoe, not a shovel."

David seemed inspired. "I want a department-head meeting scheduled for seven in the morning. I want you two to attend and Al Parker standing by to be called in." They said nothing, only stared at him. He said, "Any questions?"

David was heading for the door when Grace said, "Seven a.m.? The department heads don't get in before nine."

"Well then, we'll just give them an opportunity to find a company to work for that lets them do that. Make me up a list of department heads by longevity in office, starting with the longest."

After a day of grumbling when everybody got the memo, the last one into the meeting arrived at the stroke of seven twenty-five. David glared at the man. "Is your alarm clock broken, Jenkins?"

"No, sir, it was, you know... the traffic."

"Everybody else is here, and they came through the same traffic as you. You get three strikes in this outfit. Consider yourself as having had one." A silence as quiet as the tomb followed. Only the slightest shuffling of feet was heard.

Now David addressed the group. "Gentlemen, the meeting was scheduled for seven a.m. I won't ask who was late again, but I'm sure after you read the memo, it won't happen again under normal circumstances." Now a long and awkward silence filled the room. David cleared his throat and said, "Al Parker has given me some disturbing information."

One department head said, "Who's Al Parker?"

"He's the man you'll be working for," he said as he hit the intercom button. Speaking into the it, David said, "Al, come on in and meet your new employees."

Al entered the room. David's eyes swiveled around the conference table like a twin-mounted gun turret. "Al is the first person the morning shift meets. He tells me he has never seen any of you. As it seems you DHs have a lot of spare time early in the morning, I think it would be a good time to meet our employees. Starting tomorrow, all DHs will work a two-hour shift each morning from six thirty to eight thirty under Al's supervision. All DHs will rotate through the schedule five times. Al will fill in your time cards. Grace will have them collected at nine thirty. Okay, all back to work."

There was a general malaise, a shuffling of feet, and slow movement. As they were still moving about, David gave Grace and Alice an order, "Grace, I'm going to make a sweep of the production areas today."

Alice, in an aside to Grace, muttered, "I can't imagine what the needle on the seismograph will register when this quake hits."

That morning, there was a lot of discontent on the production floor. When David entered the area, he began snooping around the various offices. He was sorting through a particularly messy office when a man named Tom growled at him. "Get out of my stuff before I kick your ass!"

Tom marched through the door just as David turned around to confront him. David held up his hands. "Sorry!"

Tom, his hands on his hips, grumbled, "Who the hell are you?" Calmly and evenly David said, "I'm David March, the new CEO."

Tom visibly began to shake. He muttered, "Boy, did I blow it. I guess I can kiss this job good-bye."

David said, "I was looking for the supervisor to show me around and saw all this. Just curious."

Tom, very sheepish now, said, "I'm Tom, the line foreman. You won't find the supervisor here very often."

"Where is he?"

Hesitant and casting furtive glances around, he mumbled, "Probably up the street. His liquid break usually takes him to his liquid lunch. He'll be back for a nap."

"So who keeps this place running?"

"I try to take care of things. We do have a damn good maintenance crew. We keep everything up and running."

Glancing about, David asked, "What's all this stuff stacked under the workstation and hanging up?"

Tom looked nervous now. "It's all the records I'm trying to get the supervisor to maintain—machine maintenance records, downtime, overtime logs, employee attendance, brag folders, notes, reminders. Stuff like that."

"Why are you doing it? That's the supervisor's job."

Tom, looking more nervous now, said, "We got to break this up. I see the super has just got back to work."

David said, "It's been very educational, and I don't think I'd do too well in an ass-kicking contest with you."

"Well, the super saw me talking to you. He'll be chewing my ass," Tom said as the supervisor approached.

The man approached David with his hand outstretched. "As soon as I got the word that you were on the floor, I left my meeting to get back here. I see you were talking to Tom. Don't pay him any mind. He's going to college nights. Thinks he knows it all, keeps telling me how to do my job."

David glowered at him. "You smell of booze. Have you been drinking on company time?" he asked as he hit the intercom button and announced, "Security to the supervisor's office."

The super was gazing blankly at David when security arrived. David said, "Escort this man for a drug test." The super's jaw went loose. He gazed blankly at David and then back at the security guy.

David hit the intercom button again. "Tom, report to the supervisor 's office." A few minutes later, Tom arrived.

David said, "I just had the supervisor escorted for a drug test. I have a feeling he won't be working here any longer. You are the new production supervisor until you screw up. It's your job to lose. Is there anyone who can step up and do your job?"

"Sure."

"You're sure he can handle the job?"

"I can teach him anything he doesn't know. I've been doing the job for the most part for a long time now. He might need some help on the administrative end, but other than that, I have every confidence in him."

"Good. I'll inform payroll of your new status. You inform them who the new line foreman is. I'll arrange getting you administrative help."

When David left the area, Tom turned to the closest man to him. "I can't believe this. He took care of a problem we've been saddled with forever"—he snapped his fingers—"and just like that."

The man said, "Do you think there's a lesson in this for you?"

"Damn straight," he said. "I can't wait to tell my professor about this."

Later that month, Alice was taking notes from David. David said, "We have a new production supervisor, and he needs admin help setting up his office. Do we have anyone?"

Alice brightened. "I've got just the person. She's only a high school grad, but she did take some business classes."

"Good. Send her down to the production supervisor 's office. How's the new admin arrangement going?"

Alice said, "Have you seen the personnel figures?"

"Yeah, I'm expecting a call from the home office about it. I'm also concerned about the supply and material figures."

Alice, rising from her chair, said, "Hate to tell you, David, but Austy already called and wants you to call back ASAP."

A few minutes later, David was on the line to Austy. Austy sounded irritated when he said, "David, I've been watching your personnel figures. What the hell's going on?"

"I'm converting Unibrothel back to Unidraulics." "What the hell does that mean?"

"To put it bluntly, some of our DHs got too liberal with their hiring and operating practices."

"You mean we have pros…"

"Yeah, but I thought Nevada would be more suitable for their profession."

Austy was laughing uproariously. "Well, I'm glad you're on top of it. Don't be bringing any STDs back to the home office now."

Lapsing serious, David said, "I've got a real concern with the material department. I'll get to the bottom directly."

A few nights later, David was relaxing in the condo, watching TV, when the phone rang. It was Ashley calling from Omaha. "Hi, babe, what's up?"

"David, we have to talk." "Problems with Mom?"

"Things aren't good here. Mom's got all her touchy-feely friends here all the time. I think some of them are living here most of the time. And I don't mind telling you, one or the other 's always trying to cop a feel. The other day, I had to almost pry this woman's hand off my boobs."

"I'm sorry, babe. How can I help?"

"Well… can I come out there and live with you and go to school in California? I think Mom will be glad to get rid of me so she can have the house to herself. I'm a bit of a spy she doesn't need around."

"If your mother agrees, I'll go along with whatever you want, Ash."

Back at work, David was going full-steam on the changes he's implementing within the company. Tom was at work with his new administrative assistant, Alex. She's about twenty-three, tall, dressed conservatively, and pretty.

David entered the super 's office and looked around. He was smiling. "Hey, guys! Boy, what a change! You can tell just by looking at the walls and desktops what your jobs are and almost what's going on at the moment."

"Thanks, boss. It's great when you can put your knowledge to good use." David hit the intercom on Tom's desk.

"Grace, schedule a department-head meeting to be held in Tom's office for seven thirty a.m. I want them to see what a supervisor 's office should look like."

Grace said, "Well, that should be an eye-opener for them. From what Alice has told me, Alex deserves a lot of credit too."

David was still on the intercom. "My memo recommending a bonus for her just hasn't gotten up the chop chain yet," David said, winking at Alex and Tom.

Grace interjected, "The memo concerning the DH meeting is going out as we speak."

David said, "Thanks, Grace."

Turning to Tom, David said, "I'm thinking of using you as our poster boy for the education program. Does the money the company gives you cover most of your tuition?"

Tom quipped, "Bullshit! What company money?" "Bullshit?"

Tom was rankled now. "The company doesn't pay for anything. Several of us are taking classes, and we submit for reimbursement but get denied due to 'no funds available.'"

David cocked his head. "How can that be? The money was allocated in the budget."

Rather solemnly Tom said, "It went somewhere. Not to us."

"Let me look into it, Tom, and I'll see what I can do." Tom said, "Want to bet a beer?"

Back at his office, David got on the intercom. "Grace, have security canvas all employees. I want the employees' copies of all educational reimbursement requests that have not been paid on my desk by morning. Schedule a department- head meeting for ten a.m."

David was sitting at the head of the conference table. Five DHs were scattered about, all looking very uncomfortable. David's glare was enough to enhance their discomfort. "It's been brought to my attention that employee educational reimbursements have not been paid." He scanned the room at the uncomfortable demeanors. "Explanation? Anybody?"

One department head said, "I didn't allow for enough money in my department budget. I used the money to cover the shortfall."

Another department head said, "I had to replace equipment. Money had to come from somewhere."

Yet another said, "Yeah, we all faced these problems. Never enough money." David had been tapping a pencil, bouncing the rubber end off the table as he listened to the lame explanations. "Let's see if I've got this right—the company has a good profit margin, but expenses aren't being paid? Any fraudulent irregularities will be subject to legal action. If this is not agreeable to you, Grace will take your two weeks' notice and resignation."

CHAPTER NINETEEN

Two weeks later, David was having a meeting in his office with a stern-looking man, a private investigator named Jerome Deacon. If anybody could be further from the cool "Sam Spade" type, it would be Deacon. He looked more like a Baptist minister looking for sin, and when he looked at you, you shriveled. He was forty-five and a veteran private investigator specializing in corporate fraud.

David was speaking and Deacon was listening. David said, "Our operating cost is much too high. I need to find the problem. I want the plant checked twenty-four seven for at least thirty days."

Deacon said, "Compliance is a good cover. It'd give us access to all areas. It'd be four men for twenty-four seven coverage."

"No problem, I'll get you all IDs. Give me the names of your four guys as soon as you know."

Deacon stood. "Great, we're in business. My contract will be couriered to you by this afternoon."

David stopped him. "One more thing—do you have an office in Omaha?" "Sure do."

David wrote some info on a slip of paper. "This is my wife's address in Omaha. I want a complete rundown on her. Send the information directly to me."

"Is there anything in particular you're looking for, Mr. March? Or should I assume the obvious—another man?"

David leveled his gaze at the man. "I don't want you to assume anything. Just check her out and see what she's doing. I don't want to make any assumptions."

Deacon's face split in the only grin David had seen on him. "Wise man."

As soon as the PI left, David got an intercom message from Grace. "David, Tom's on the phone."

"Yo, Tom."

"Guess what I got?" "Herpes?"

"Nope. Better. I got a check for twenty-five hundred dollars for my tuition. I owe you a beer. How about after work tonight?" "You're on."

That night, David and Tom were at a neighborhood bar, Tony's, having drinks. Tom had a suggestion. "How about having a sack lunch with the production crew tomorrow? You won't believe the attitude changes."

David was quick. "You're on. You involved with anyone?"

Tom looked at him funny. "Hey, wait a minute… You one of those funny guys?" David grins. "'Funny guys.' I've been accused of a lot of things and called a lot of things but never funny guy."

"You know what I mean. They play hide the sausage. But in odd places." Laughing, David told him, "Look, my stepdaughter and her friend are driving out here. They're a couple of college kids and, like most college kids, think they know it all. I need someone their age to show them around and introduce them to others their age. Would you be interested? I'll pay for the evening."

"How could I pass up a deal like that? You're on."

A while later, David was on the phone to Austy. "David, what the hell's going on now? I see a couple of key people have left."

"Yeah, they decided that they didn't want to work for a living. I'll tell you, Austy, it's a tribute to our product or some divine guidance that our company has done so well with all the crap I've found. We should be a veritable gold mine very soon now."

"I know what you mean. Figures are up over thirty-eight percent. That's phenomenal."

"I hate to brag, Austy, but if you look at the latest figures, it's closer to forty-two percent. If my hunch pays off, I'm hoping for a big increase in a couple of months."

That night, David was working at the condo when the buzzer rang. He answered.

"It's us. We're here," Ashley said. "Chill out. I'll be right down."

Ashley's friend was a gorgeous and vivacious twenty-three-year-old named Brenda. But as far as David was concerned, it could have been Goddess.

Ashley hugged David and gave him a quick peck on the cheek.

Brenda was all smiles. "When Ashley asked me to help with the driving, I couldn't pass up the opportunity."

Still enthralled, David said, "Let's get your luggage unloaded."

Brenda said, "I've heard so much about this place, I can't wait to see it."

As Ashley showed her friend around, there was a plethora of oohs and aahs and wows.

David appeared with a platter of drinks. "How about drinks on the patio, ladies?"

Ashley was thrilled acting the tour guide and was eagerly pointing out the landmarks to her friend.

David said, "I'm sorry, girls, I've been so busy I haven't planned out anything for this evening. I—"

Ashley interrupted. "Cool it. I've got it all planned. The three of us will do Chinatown and the Edinburgh Castle. It's Friday, so the bagpiper will be there, and for breakfast…"

David grinned. "Let me guess, the Cliff House?" Ashley added, "And the big Johnson."

"But I do have tomorrow night planned. I have a college guy that's going to show you where the young crowd hangs out."

Brenda and Ashley exchanged happy grins.

It's a typical Bay Area night. The fog had long burned off, and the evening cool was coming off the bay. Whitecaps danced in the gentle breeze. Ashley, Brenda, and David were strolling atop Russian Hill, which offered the most panoramic, sweeping view of the bay, the bridge, and Alcatraz Island.

Brenda was particularly enthralled. She said, "I need to spend some time here. I see a lot of neat gifts to take back home." Ashley said, "You have two weeks."

David was happy to play tour guide. Soon they found themselves at the Edinburgh Castle on Geary Street near the water. It was twilight, and the stars were coming out. Brenda said, "Ashley's told me so much about this place I feel like I've been here."

David said, "You can find Irish pubs in any city in America, but how many Scots pubs can you find? This place is unique. Not only does it look so much like an authentic Scots castle with all the authentic tapestries and artifacts, but it also might as well be in Edinburgh."

Brenda, awed, said, "It's so great!"

"But the culture is here too," David commented, enjoying the tour leader role himself. "The castle is home to the Scottish Cultural and Arts Foundation. It always attracts a brilliant author's reading and other stuff. For big names, they've had Irvine Weish, and Patrick McCabe. Of course, our own local Alan Black, manager of the castle."

When the Scottish dancing came on, complete with bagpipers in full kilts, all three of them joined the circle of dancers. David, laughing, said, "Nothing like it to get the blood flowing."

After they sat down, Ashley and Brenda, still puffing from the vigorous go- round, wanted a drink. Ashley said, "Wait till you try this Laphroaig."

Brenda giggled. "Lap who?"

"Laphroaig, a fine malt liquor. It'll wash down the fish and chips just great." After a round of darts, they felt that they had truly experienced a piece of Scotland.

In the morning, they found themselves at the Cliff House, having brunch washed down with champagne. The Cliff House was perched on a high cliff on the western side of San Francisco, overlooking the site of the old Sutro Baths.

Gazing down at the water, David said, "Lots of ships got pounded to pieces below this cliff on many a stormy night."

Brenda said, "The view is beyond belief. What's those rocks out there?" Ashley piped in. "Seal rocks. See all the seals?"

When, later, they went upstairs to the omelet bar for their Big Johnson, Brenda remarked, "Big Johnson has a whole different meaning back in Omaha. It only took me twenty-four hours to lose my heart in San Francisco."

David smiled. "When we get done here, you guys can drop me off at the condo and go exploring. That's more fun, finding your own favorite spots. Now don't forget your escort is picking you up at seven. Remember, this is the college crowd. You don't need pilot dresses."

Brenda did a double take. "Pilot dresses?"

Ashley rolled her eyes and said, "I'll tell you later."

David was sitting up in bed, reading, when the girls got home. He greeted them with a cheery "Hi, roomies, come in and tell me all about your night on the town."

They came into his room and sat at the foot of the bed. Ashley was still swooning. "That Tom is a dream."

Brenda added, "It was an experience. College kids are sure different out here. I thought I was on a different planet. It isn't fair. I get to go to Omaha, and Ashley gets Tom."

David grinned. "Well, my parental duty is done, you're home, and I can go to sleep. So scat." Ashley gave David a chaste peck on the cheek.

But Brenda said, "I'm not related, I can do better than that." She kissed David passionately, her tongue seeking his. As they left, Brenda first, Ashley looked over her shoulder and wiggled her finger back and forth while shaking her head. She said, "I'll be down a little later."

CHAPTER TWENTY

David planned to meet his PI later that day, and he found himself in a commercial building. He stopped at a door marked Coast to Coast and he entered. Jerome Deacon was ready with a hearty handshake. He motioned David to follow him. "My office is back here."

David had built up a good deal of angst by now. He knew he was going to hear something he didn't want to.

"Let's go to the business part first. We got something formulated for your chop. It seems your production department head has a special thing called flex employees. There are people that are authorized entrance to the manufacturing complex at any time. They even come in on weekends. Ever hear of such devoted employees?"

"Let me guess—they carry stuff out?"

"That's right. Not only for themselves, but who knows what they're selling to the competition?"

"Thank goodness our products are extremely difficult to reverse engineer. Got any ideas on how to stop it?"

"Yeah, sure do. It's a one-way off the main street in the hourly employee's parking lot. They exit at the other end of the lot back onto the one-way street. The island prevents anyone from coming in the exit. On a Saturday morning, we propose blocking the exit gate for the weekend with a dummy construction job, making everyone exit through the executive parking lot on the other side of the complex. Everyone will be stopped at the gate for a vehicle search. Anyone caught will be turned over to the police. Don't be surprised if your production department head is one of them. He's got a little project going on."

"Sounds like a plan. When do we implement it?"

Deacon handed David a list. He said, "I'd like you to arrange a big purchase for these items. We'll set the sting for the first Saturday and Sunday after the delivery."

Back at the condo that night, David was sipping a drink while Ashley was working on her laptop. Suddenly she stopped typing and turned to David. "David, do you know how much I like Tom?"

"How many guesses do I get?" She stuck her tongue out at him.

He said, "He's here so much I was beginning to think he lived here."

"He asked me to move in with him." She waited for a reaction, secretly hoping for a big protest, but that's not what she got.

David did stop drinking and take a quick breath. "Uh." "So what would you say if I did?"

David, his jaw a bit opened, said, "You're an adult, Ash. Follow your heart. If it feels right, do it. I'll get over the empty-nest thing."

"What about the empty-bed thing?"

He looked sad enough to make a sobering remark, but instead he said, "Well, when in Russia, do as the Russians do."

She grinned. "Yeah, find another yeppie?"

David was watching from his office window as multiple vehicles were being searched by the security guards. Some people were being put in police squad cars.

Later that afternoon, Deacon was in David's office. "Well," he said, sounding satisfied, "looks like we made a complete sweep. Any more thieves and you'd be cleaned out." He lapsed more serious as he turned to David. "Now about that Omaha report you wanted."

David said, "Let's have a look at it before you leave the case. I need something else."

"It's all pretty straightforward. Your wife is involved in pretty intense associations with the lesbian and bisexual community. They show some activity at your house, and here are the names and addresses. I don't mean to be frivolous, sir, but those girls are going at it day and night."

David, though somber, said, "Great job on both contracts. Thanks for everything. Please submit your bill, and it will be paid promptly."

David was taking a few moments to gaze out his window—something he rarely did, except sometimes when he got a premonition, and when the phone rang, he had one. It was Julia. She had already been confronted, and she maintained a civil tone.

"David, some bad news on this end. Dad died. If you come back for the funeral, you can stay with Mom."

Before David could formulate something to say, the phone went dead.

Hazel and David, both dressed in black, were home from the funeral. Hazel was in a contemplative mood. David thought that was natural enough but not her next statement. She said, "I hate to say this, but I almost feel relieved. These last few years have been like living among the living dead."

David said, "When you get all the loose ends tied up, take that San Francisco trip you always wanted. Come out and stay with me until you get things sorted out."

She said nothing, but he had a good idea that she was considering it.

A month later, David and Hazel were in bed making love, when suddenly the door burst open and Ashley was in the room. The young woman's jaw dropped. She slumped to the foot of the bed. David's voice was rather pathetic as he bleated out, "Ash."

The return by Hazel was more shocking. "Let's get real, Ashley. Are you really shocked by David and me having sex, or is it because it's not you and David?"

Ashley, sobbing, said, "Grandma, how could you say such a thing?"

Hazel was tight lipped. "How dumb do you think I am? I knew that you and David were having sex when you came back from Russia. You were a very different person when you returned—all of a sudden, you were more sensitive and gentle, and not to mention, you never missed a chance to cozy up to him."

David let out a long sigh. "Now that that's out in the open, what now?"

Hazel was first to speak. "Ashley, I love you with all my heart. You and I need to talk about the wonderful blessing we both share. When I'm with David, it is the only time I feel like the woman I want to be. That must describe your feelings too."

There's a long silence. Then Ashley got up and wordlessly left the room.

In the morning, David and Hazel were eating breakfast. The mood was somber. David asked, "What do you want your life to be like in the future?"

"I'd like a big change for a while. I've got mixed emotions about my house and living in it."

"Well, there's no reason to rush anything. Just be sure you're going to something and not running away from something."

"I'm so concerned about Ashley and what she really feels."

David put down his coffee cup. "I am too. How about you staying here until you and Ashley recreate that bond you had in the past?"

Now it was Hazel's turn to sigh. "I don't have any friends here. I don't know how to act or live in a big city."

"I can always help you get Kalifornianized." "You can't mean what I think you mean?" Innocently David said, "What?"

"A paid escort? No, it'd make me feel cheap." "Then let me think on it."

Later, in the master bathroom, David was shaving, and Hazel was applying her makeup. He said, "Oh, by the way, I invited Ashley and Tom for a catered dinner this evening."

"Anything special I need to do?"

He smiled and said, "No, just be your wonderful self."

One evening, while Hazel was straightening out the living room, the buzzer rang. She thought it was Ashley, and she said, "Come on up, Ash."

Ed Rolf answered, "I know I'm old, but I'm not ashes yet."

Hazel asked. "You're who? David didn't say—Oh, I'm so sorry."

David came to the intercom. "Come on up, Ed." David turned to Hazel. "It's Ed Rolf. I invited him to dinner." He turned to the intercom. "Hi, Ed. I got this cranky old woman up here. She uses a broom for transportation. I'll send her down. Her broom rides double."

When Ed and Hazel emerged from the elevator, they were laughing. David said, "Hi, Ed. Now, Hazel, you could stand here while I tell Ed about you. And Ed could just stand here while I tell you about him. But then that would take away all your talking points.

"So I'll freshen Hazel's drink and fix you one, Ed, and the two of you can go out on the balcony and tell lies to each other."

They barely heard him as they walked out to the balcony to be served the drinks when David had them ready.

Just then, Ashley and Tom arrived. David said, "Hi, guys."

Ashley said, "How's Grandma getting along with Ed?"

David pointed to the balcony and said, "See for yourselves." Ashley murmured, "Kalifornianized."

Later that evening, David and Hazel were in bed. Hazel said, "Ed invited me to spend a day with him exploring Marin County."

"You and Ed seem to have a great emotional connection. If you need help with the physical stuff, you know where to come."

"That physical stuff—I think I could use some now." David turned off the lights and moved toward her.

Next morning, David was talking to Grace. She said, "With the production department head on paid leave from being caught up in the thief sting, what now?"

David said, "Oh, Grace, what to do, what to do? I know what I want to do. It's a risk, but I have a good feeling about it." For once, he wasn't kidding around.

"I don't know what it is, but I say follow your gut. Everything you've done so far has vastly improved this company."

"I'm just thinking of putting Tom in that position on a temp basis."

Grace said, "You've had him train department heads and supervisors. With his education and a little more insight into the other business aspects, he'd be ready to take your place. You've been telling everyone that their first responsibility is to identify their relief."

"That settles it. I'm going down to see Tom. Talk to Alice, I want Alex to make the move with him."

David was talking to Austy on the phone, who was saying, "David, the figures I have in front of me show your profits are up over one hundred and twenty-five percent. I need you back here for a strategy session. Plan on a week, maybe a little longer."

Later, Hazel said, "Ed asked me to take an around-the-world trip with him." David said, "So?"

"Do you think it would be okay?"

David smiled. "Follow your heart, darling, follow your heart."

She smiled. "Well, it feels right." Then she hesitated. "I know—if it feels right, do it."

"I have to go back to the home office for about a week. Can you hold off until I get back?"

In Omaha, David and Austy were in a meeting. Austy said, "David, I want to expand our business into other areas. I want you to head up a new special projects department. It would mean moving back here."

David lapsed deep in thought. "Can you give me a little time to get my head around the concept? I'd like a couple of weeks to put some ideas together for us to kick around before we jump in."

"That's a good idea. By the way, you're staying in a motel? Everything okay with Julia?"

"Staying in a motel. That should give you your answer. Our marriage was over years ago, just haven't tied up the loose ends. When I get back here, it will all be resolved very quickly. No impact."

Austy put down his glass and leveled his gaze at David. "That leads me to believe that you've accepted the job."

"I like everything about it. I just want you and me to go through a little brainstorming before we jump in, make sure we're on the same page. In fact, I have a few ideas right now if you have time."

An hour later, Austy said, "I agree with your ideas. Kicking it off hosting a world conference should fill up our think tank. It'll reap vast rewards. Speaking of vast rewards, the board knows you deserve a huge one. I mean, a multimillion- dollar one. However, with the prospects of laying out large sum to expand, they feel the need to preserve capital. It just isn't right."

"I'll be upfront with you. Yes, I do deserve a large bonus, and I understand the board's feelings. Austy, what if I come up with a way to give me a bonus that doesn't require any money to change hands?"

"They won't go for giving you Unidraulics!"

"No, but how about the San Francisco condo?"

Austy said, "That's it. I'll make arrangements for the deed transfer."

A few days later, Hazel was doing the dishes when David walked through the front door.

He said, "I'm being transferred back to Omaha." "Omaha? That was quick."

"No, the home office and I have been working on it for some time. The board of directors couldn't pay me the bonus that I deserve, so they gave me this condo."

"But you won't be here? Are you going to rent it out?" "I thought I'd let Ash and Tom live here."

"What a wonderful gift."

David said, "Why don't you give Ash a call and invite her and Tom? We'll have some drinks here and then go out to eat. I think she and Tom are going to love the news."

Next morning, back at the office, David was talking to Julia in Omaha. "I'm being transferred back to Omaha, Julia."

Julia was in bed, her lover, Beth, beside her. Julia asked, "How soon?" "As soon as I wrap things up here."

"Where are you going to live?" "In my house."

Her voice rising several decibels, she screamed, "That's not possible! You've been away for so long I've turned this into a social headquarters for all my women's clubs. See if Mom will let you stay at her house."

Back in San Francisco, Hazel was packing for her trip with Ed Rolf.

She was a bit maudlin. "It's sad. This will be our last night together for a long time. Ed is talking about spending time in a lot of different places."

"Good or bad?"

"Oh, David, all good. If it was you and me, I would have said excellent."

CHAPTER TWENTY-ONE

Later, back in Austy's office, David and Austy were formulating plans. Austy said, "I like the format. We'll go with it—a world-manufacturing conference right here in Omaha."

"It will take time to put it all together."

Later, David was working on his computer in the Omaha office. When the phone beeped, David picked up the phone and read a text from Ashley.

"Tom asked me to marry him. I said yes."

David typed on the phone, "What does this mean for us?" "No more yeppie."

After he had written the yeppie remark, David had a conversation with himself. Isn't it odd that my first reaction to something that should make Ashley, whom I love, happy is that I am going to lose her? And let's face it, I am thinking mostly sexually. I have to be honest with myself about that. We're of two different generations. What, other than sex, do we have in common? Why, it almost seems degenerate the way she used to cling to my hand on trips to Disney World and other places. She had been my little girl. Until she grew up and became my lover. Was everything about his love life perverse? he had to ask himself, and not rhetorically either.

It's true that Ashley had always talked about her mother not deserving him and that she did, but he never encouraged that. He never promised her anything. Yet here he was, shocked that she had found someone of her own age to live with and love and be happy with. He had never even imagined losing Ashley to someone else. Oh sure, he encouraged her to go out with people her own age, but that was his parental duty. Not something he really—not deep down in his heart—wanted. It's true that he was always attracted to her. She was young, bold, and flirtatious. Who could resist? Especially when they were alone together so much. And he had another odd feeling about Ashley.

Considering women's intuition, it was hard to believe that Julia had no reason to suspect the two. The trip to Russia and many other occasions—was it Julia's way of getting him a girlfriend to keep him out of her hair?

Later, in an Omaha lawyer's office, an attorney was advising David. "She'll want everything you have."

"Well, let's just deliver the divorce papers to Mrs. March and wait for a response."

Back at her Omaha house, Julia was furiously tearing at a certified letter she just signed for. She snapped at Beth, "Divorce papers!"

Beth grabbed the papers and quickly perused them.

"He names me as the cause! How did he find out about me?"

"Ashley! We must not have been as discreet as we thought. Oh no! There are pictures, names, and addresses. Here's a list of all the gals that are married."

Beth paled. "Oh my gosh, what's gonna happen to them? I have to warn them. "God, Julia, a lot of the girls are married, and their husbands don't know they're bisexual."

Julia jumped in. "Some of them know. They even get into it with them." Julia rambled on. "He's asking for the property. Beth, he's suing for a quarter of a million dollars. For alienation of affection. Well, a lawyer will make quick work of that. I'll show him. I'll countersue for everything he's got."

Back in his office, David was working when the phone rang. It was Hazel. She sounded different. Her voice was a combination of awe and excitement. "David, Ed and I are married!"

"Married? That was quick." David was beginning to feel abandoned. "David, please be happy for me, would you?"

"That's not the kind of would you I'd like to hear."

Hazel sounded earnest now. "Please tell me how you really feel. It's important to me."

"It's what I've always said, darling. Follow your heart. If it feels right, do it." Hazel's marriage hit a different and new chord in David's melody of life. He had always considered Hazel his—even more than a wife, someone who would always be there. Someone who was—well, he hated to say it but—almost a personal possession. She needed him, and he certainly needed her. Imagine, he would choose a young wife's mother over the young wife.

Any first-year college student in psychology 101 could see the answer, but David was so close to the situation that he did not.

Since he never had a sexual experience with Julia before they were married, he had no idea what to expect. He was just so very happy to have her that he didn't rate the sex. That she was his—that he had her—was enough. Soon, sexual performance, as rare as it was, seemed to make no difference in their lives. After all, he was having outstanding sex with Hazel and even getting to be the big city slicker and teach her things. Then there was young, luscious, voluptuous Ashley. Who could resist a beautiful young woman with all her vibrancy and joie de vivre? She didn't need a romantic location for her first sex with David. An Eskimo igloo would have been good enough although a dumpy Russian hotel room wasn't that far off.

Now she belonged to someone else. He thought maybe he could get Hazel to cheat on Ed with him, but he didn't want that. It would cheapen everything that went before, although through most peoples' eyes, the affair they had been carrying on for years was just short of incest.

Was Hazel the wife he never had? The woman who thought he was not only a great guy but also a stud in bed? And worldly—he taught her things she had never really even heard of. Did that swell his ego? Was that what every man wanted his wife to think of him rather than the American icon of Dagwood Bumstead or the Family Guy?

David's problem with Julia was that he never realized that she was gay. Oh, she could do a man if she had to, just as she did with him. But it was definitely lacking. It was the softness of a woman's flesh that she craved, that got her off. Not the hard, angular, hairy body of a man. These things tended to move David off his normal sexual guidance system and confused the hell out of him.

"Go easy on the matressonomy stuff. You don't want his old ticker to stop ticking."

He was trying to be funny, but funny was the last thing he felt. He had a tremendous feeling of loss. Hazel had been a fixture in his life. She had been the kingpin, even more than Ashley, who was bound to find someone her own age.

That afternoon, Julia was on the phone to her lawyer. He was saying, "Unless you and your husband can come to some agreement, you stand to lose everything." Julia flared up. "What? What happened to every day is Mother's Day in the Nebraska judicial system?"

"Not with what he's got on you. He's got you in bed not with one but multiple women. That stuff doesn't go over in conservative Nebraska."

Julia picked up a nearby phone and dialed David. "David, it's me. Can we meet at the club for lunch tomorrow?"

The next day, they were sitting at their usual table, being served by their usual waiter. Julia had developed a more reasonable tone of voice. She gazed at him over the rim of her martini glass. "For old times' sakes—and there were some good times—is there any chance we can work something, some kind of settlement?"

"Yeah, we can. Your mother is married. I'll buy her house and give it to you. You can rent rooms to your tit-suckers."

Julia sniffled. It might have been genuine. "How can you be so mean?"

David pulled a package of pictures out of his briefcase and spread them on the table. Holding out his arms, palms up in a stay-away motion, he said to her, "You can never go back."

She was putting on the charm now, giving him that killer smile of hers and reaching for his hand and caressing it softly. "Look, I truly thought that you knew something about me. I didn't think you'd have married me if you were completely in the dark. I never intended to take time away from you and give it to my friends. I am who I am, and I thought we could all get along. I wouldn't deny you anything, and you, in turn, would allow me my occasional escapades. I mean, if you look at it logically, I'm not screwing another man. No man is putting his penis in me."

"You expect any ordinary man to accept that?" "Well, I guess I didn't think of you as ordinary."

David stared over her head. "Is there any possibility you could give up this lifestyle altogether?"

Now she thought awhile. "To save our marriage, I believe I could."

David sipped some more of his martini. "You know how hard it is for me to believe that. Your ex hinted that you guys did all kinds of things, including with guys."

"I won't deny that, but I'm not into that. I'll be involved to a certain extent, but no intercourse." During this silence she put on her salesman hot. "Look, David, life isn't like when we were growing up. People are experimenting, getting into different things. To me, more marriages have been saved than lost by it too."

"We have our daughter to think of too."

David now felt a pang of his own guilt. He wondered. Who am I, acting holier- than-thou? And that isn't even counting Hazel.

She added, "Would you at least think about it? I now know exactly how you feel, and I'll withdraw from the active lifestyle. Will that give us a chance?"

He wondered how odd life was. Here was the girl of his dreams, whom he finally got to marry, begging him to keep their marriage together. Her face still thrilled him. He still was awed by what he considered her perfection. And what do I know about gay people? Who am I to judge them in any way? God knows I've made my own sins in this life—for whatever reason, for whatever and however I justified it. Maybe I should give her another chance.

David sipped his martini and smacked his lips. "I truly don't think that what you're doing is a choice but something that was born into you. I don't know if that's a popular definition or not, but maybe we can work something out. I have to go to South America on a job, and if you would wait for an answer, I'll think it all out and give you my answer when I get back. Would that be okay?"

She smiled—that smile he loved. "It's fine with me, and, darling, I do think we can work it out. We've both made our share of mistakes in life. Let's try again."

That ended the conversation, and David went back to the office to prepare for the troubleshooting trip to Venezuela. It made him feel good about trying to work it out. It somehow made him feel more noble than he actually was. He was willing to try again with this girl who had consumed his life and his thoughts since his youth.

In Tom and Ashley's new condo given to them by David, Tom was sitting on the couch, looking over his and Ashley's wedding photos. Ashley entered, looking pale, and she was trembling. Tom jumped up and went to her. "What's wrong, sweetheart? What's happened?"

"I need to be myself before I can talk to you."

Ashley left the living room to her bedroom. Tom paced the floor, waiting for Ashley to come out of the bedroom. Eventually, she emerged. She said to him, "Here, sit on the couch beside me."

They sat down and Ashley, now crying, said, "This is hard, Tom. I love you with all my heart, but I'm pregnant!"

Tom, beaming, said, "That's great, honey." Ashley's face dropped. "It may not be yours." Now his face turned pale. "Not mine?"

"It might be David's. The reason I'm telling you is that I love you and don't want to deceive you, and the truth comes out anyway. I want the baby to know who his father is. I'll respect any decision you make. The only request I make is, if it's a boy, his name will be David."

Tom sat for a while, gazing off into space. "I'm stunned! But I respect your honesty. We'll live it day by day for a while."

In a large conference hall, David was addressing an international conference. He was saying, "We've had two very productive and informative days. Tomorrow will be a free day with no structured meetings on our part. Please seek out your counterparts in companies from different countries around the world. As an aid, we have the names posted by positions and companies and lodging."

Back at David's office, he was sitting at his desk. Framed pictures of Julia, Hazel, and Ashley were sitting in front of him. David picked up one and slowly rubbed his hand across the face in the picture. As he reached for the next picture, tears started running down his face. Rubbing the face in the picture, he put it down, and he picked up the next one. He repeated this again with each picture.

When the door opened, David whipped the chair around so his back was to the door, hiding him and his emotions from view. His secretary was standing in the doorway, curious about the slight heaving of his shoulders.

"David, there is a lady waiting to see you." "Have her wait. I'll be finished here shortly."

David composed himself and spoke into the intercom. "Send in the lady that is waiting."

In walked a gorgeous tall blonde—a green-eyed vision. It was his Pam from New Zealand.

She smiled and said, "Do you have a few minutes for an old Kiwi love?" "Pam! I didn't know you were here!"

"I'm only here as a recorder for one company." "You should have contacted me sooner."

"I thought, since we have the day off, you and I might be able to spend some time together."

"Might? Hell, we will!"

They were having dinner at one of his favorite restaurants when a revelation came to him. He said, "Seeing you again has made me realize something."

"What?" With a good natured grin, she said, "Get rid of the girl-friends when an old girlfriend comes to town?"

Not taking the bait and dead serious, he said, "We work hard so that we can take care of those we love. When I promised you I could help you and take care of you if need be, I wasn't lying. But I wasn't telling the truth either."

She put down her martini glass, her eyes dilated.

"No, I knew I was going places and would at least be a financial success. But I was just hoping. Money will buy you houses and yachts and trips. But the most important is the financial security you can give your loved ones. Now I am in a position to help my loved ones."

She put her glass down and hesitated. "You mean... I..." "Yes, you certainly are a loved one."

The happiness on her face was worth any and every sacrifice he had ever made in life.

"Maybe we could even plan a few days together in the future. Any special place?"

They exchanged a silly glance, faces lit up! They chorused in unison, "Hawaii, Davy Jones Locker."

David got on his intercom. "Hold all calls, I'm leaving for the day."

Later they were sitting in Davy Jones Locker, looking out into the deep end of the swimming pool, swimmers standing outside on the edge, adjusting themselves. "David and Pam in Davy Jones Locker, looking out," she said. "What's so great about reliving old times?"

"Old times are fun. They put you back with someone you were happy with at a happy time."

CHAPTER TWENTY-TWO

Outside, on the sunny balcony at Honolulu Airport, amid the soft breeze and faint odor of jet fumes, Pam lingered in David's arms, reluctant to let go. She was teary-eyed. "Oh, David, I hate good-byes, especially this one. It was so good to be with you again. Let's say good-bye here. Don't walk me to the Jetway."

"Are you sure?"

She looked up, raising her long-lashed eyes to him. "Yes, I'm sure." Fluttering her lashes, she murmured, "When I'm overwhelmed, I'll call you to rescue me. Deal?"

"Deal. Remember, you're my favorite Kiwi. I'll never forget you."

She started for the exit, daring one last peek at him over her shoulder as she left. He waited until she was gone.

Back at work, David was still a bit distracted when the phone rang. "Hi, Ash, what's up?"

Her voice was more earnest than usual. "I asked Mom to come out for a visit. I can't hide the truth any longer."

Blowing through his teeth, he said, "She'll blow her top when she finds out I'm the baby's father."

"Well, to be honest, my feeling is that Mom wanted me to take her place. So that will be my defense. Anyway, after Mom discovers the San Francisco gay scene, she will fixate on that."

"What about Tom?"

"We're living apart but talking things through. It had hurt him so bad. He was really looking forward to his own child."

With a sigh, David said, "Well, I guess it's time I open up a line of communication with Tom. I probably owe him at least that much. Frankly, I think he's nuts, letting a beautiful girl like you get away."

"That'll be his call, but I'm sure he'll be open to talking to you. After all, he owes his career to you."

David's eyes wandered to the clock. Time to hit the club.

The bar was dim and sedate as usual. A woman approached him as he took his first sip. Grinning, she asked, "Got an extra drink in your pocket?"

Smiling, he said, "Sure, Ann. You're usually here with your husband."

Sitting down beside him, she crossed her legs in a whisper of silk and said, "He's out of town. Seems to be out of town more than in town."

"Everything okay between you two?"

"I'm not sure yet, but I suspect some hanky-panky." With a grin, David said, "His or yours?"

"Both, I suspect."

"I arrived at the same conclusion sometime ago."

Now it was her turn to sigh. "Yeah, that information made the circuit in a hurry." "So now here we are hanging out at the bar."

She sipped her drink and eyed him through her peripherals and murmured, her voice sultry, "Are you up to party?"

David only had to think for a moment. "Will I know anyone?" "No, but how long that is depends on you."

She took his arm, and he hurried to finish his drink. "I know just the place. My friends have these little get-together parties. My husband won't go, so I'm always left out."

"Well, let's change all that."

They stopped at a liquor store for a bottle and headed for the party. Several couples were mingling, and the music was soft. Most greeted Ann.

A guy who looked ripped in a sports jacket said, "I see you finally ditched that old fart and found someone to party with."

They began to mingle, Ann introducing David around. There were soft music and slow dancing and an erotic expectation in the air. The hostess, a knockout blonde in a backless dress with a slit up her thigh, called out, "All men to the rec room."

Another woman called, "Wait, we have a stranger, and I don't feel comfortable. We don't know him."

A grinning Ann, hugging David's arms, said, "I'll vouch for him. He's with me." The men then headed for the rec room and then closed the door.

Back in the living room, the women tossed their car keys in a pile on the floor and left the house. Then the hostess called, "Okay, guys, charge!"

The men hurried out of the room and dove into the pile of car keys. After each one had a key, he headed for the door.

The women were standing by their cars as the men ran from car to car, trying to unlock them. Horns honked as remotes were actuated. When a door unlocked, the woman standing beside it and the man would get in and drive off.

Ann grabbed David's arm. "Okay, David, it's off to your place. I'm not playing their little game tonight. Why should I take a chance that someone else will get you?"

At his place, David took his hosting duties seriously and made sure Ann got the drink of her preference and was comfortable. "How often do you have these parties?"

"Monthly mostly but the numbers change due to women having their period. It's our own little swingers club," she said as she let her dress drop to her ankles. He quickly got her out of her bra and panties.

David was still thinking about it at his desk in the morning when the phone rang. "David, this is Gail. We met last night at the party. From what I'm told, you're my kind of partner. Can we meet for a naked lunch?"

Grinning, he said, "What do you mean you've been told?"

"That's the rule. After each party, the women submit a report on their partner's performance. You got a triple A, so you'll be receiving a few more calls. Keep a lot of reloads on hand."

Ashley and Julia were sipping wine on the balcony. All of San Francisco lay before them, with the Golden Gate in the distance, shimmering in the setting sun. Julia crossed her legs and said, "Now what's this important thing you have to tell me?"

Ash was tentative. She took another sip before she spoke. "Mom, now please keep an open mind. The baby... uh, well, it's not Tom's. David is the father."

Julia's eyes dilated. She leaped to her feet so fast that she almost dropped her drink. "You and David? When? How?"

Ash was now cool. "When you abandoned him as his wife and me as your daughter, we both turned to each other for emotional support. From there, things just turned physical."

"Whe-when did this start?"

"The sex started when we were in Russia. Remember, you refused to go. David and I suspect you wanted me to take your place as his wife so you could live your other life."

Julia cocked her head and stared at her daughter. "What... what makes you think I needed anyone to take my place?"

"Because you basically abandoned him, left him on his own in favor of your lesbian friends."

Julia was still sputtering. "Why did I ever let you get that close to that son of a bitch!"

Ashley now put her hand out. "Don't, Mom! Don't go there. I won't let you talk about David like that. David is the most loving, caring man I know. You remember my frustration with men—or should I say boys—whose idea of foreplay was a sniff 'n' mount? Well, David taught me love and tenderness and the joy of sexual satisfaction. You threw him away when you decided to become a lesbian."

Julia cast her eyes down, her demeanor changed. It took her a while, but eventually she said, "Please don't judge me like that. I didn't choose to be a lesbian. From a very young age, I was confused, never understanding my sexuality. Only after I experienced the physical love of another woman did I understand my sexuality. Yes, Ashley, I did cheat David out of all those years when he should have had a loving partner. I so badly needed the lifestyle he afforded me. I was selfish, and regardless of what you think, every day of my life I regret what I did to David. I would very much like to be friends with him."

Ashley looked askance, puzzled. Julia said, "What about Tom?"

"We have very deep feelings for each other. He just can't get past what happened between David and me. We're living apart, trying to work things out."

At the condo, Ashley handed the baby over to the nanny. As Ash and Julia headed out the door, Ashley said, "We'll do a quick tour of the city, hit some trendy places and then onto the Castro District. You'll equate."

Soon they were mingling in a teeming gay area of the city, and Julia's interest was more than piqued—she gazed about in utter fascination. She mingled with the crowd, exchanging flirting glances and giggles. Eventually mother and daughter stopped for tea and biscuits.

Julia sipped her tea, her eyes still roaming. "I feel so comfortable here. Yes, I equate. Ashley, can I hang here for a while? Give me some money to get back to the condo."

"I'll do better than that. I'll have my driver take me back and have him come and post up right here. Just tell him what you want from him. He's yours for the rest of the day."

Back at the condo that evening, the pair was working on dinner while sipping a new Napa Valley wine. Julia muttered, "And I used to hate California. I guess I just didn't see all of it."

Ashley asked, "So you really love San Francisco?"

Chopping celery for the salad, Julia said, "I can see me and Beth living in the Castro District. I saw where a travel agency had gay-and lesbian-tours. What fun that would be!"

When the phone rang, Ash picked it up, listened, and handed it to her mother. "Mom, it's Grandma."

Wiping her hands on a dishtowel, Julia said, "Hi, Mom." Laughing, Hazel said, "What are you doing in my city?"

Julia laughed. "The part I like, I don't think you would call your town. Where are you calling from anyway?"

"I'm calling from my chateau in Switzerland. It's so beautiful here. Like a painting. You need to come for a visit. And yes, you can bring Beth."

In David's office, the phone seemed extra loud in the quiet. "Hi, Pam, What am I doing? Just boring paperwork."

"Just checking in. Haven't talked to you since Hawaii. Coming back to New Zealand was a good decision. England was great and fun, but I love my New Zealand. You can take the Kiwi out of the country, but you can't take the Kiwi out of the girl."

"Isn't Hawaii on your favorite list too?"

Giggling, she said, "I'll always be ready for a shot of Davy Jones Locker. Of course, who can forget Davy Jones Locker and that pool full of bare asses? I'll see it again someday. Well, back to work. Great talking to you."

David hung up and sat gazing into space, a twinkle in his eyes.

The chateau in Switzerland, built in the Tyrolean style, cast its shadow on the lake, in the distance, the Alps, snow covered and jagged. Ed, gasping for breath, staggered out of the pool and lunged at a lounge chair.

Later, Hazel, arranging flowers around the patio area, checked her watch and began looking for Ed. She discovered him lying on the tile floor of the patio in distress. Evidently, he never made it to the lounge chair. Hazel screamed and rushed to him. With one hand to her lips she touched his body. He was cold. It's obvious he was dead.

Most of the staff of Unidraulics Corporation and old business associates attended the funeral, as well as Ed's extended family. It was a sad affair since Ed seemed to have a lot of life to live yet.

Back at the Marin County home a few weeks later, David was comforting Hazel. She leaned her head on his shoulder and hung on to his arm. She murmured, "I'll have to depend on you to help me settle his estate. It's much too complicated for me, and I don't trust most lawyers."

Rifling through her papers, David said, "It looks pretty simple. Ed left everything to you."

Hazel looked startled. "What about his grandchildren?"

David looked at the papers again for a moment. "Here's a notarized statement that certifies that the kids already got their inheritance. The estate is worth close to a billion dollars. If you feel generous, you can do something more for his grandchildren. In fact, I suggest that you do."

Later in the lawyer 's office, Hazel, David, and Ed's three young adult grandchildren were present. The lawyer, in an officious tone, began speaking. "Your stepgrandmother has instructed me to do something very special for you three. I'm instructed to pay off any debts you have. Also after ten years, if you live healthy, productive lives, each of you will receive one million dollars."

The three rushed to Hazel and started gushing. "Grandma, you're so wonderful." Another said, "That's more than I could ever have hoped for." Yet another said, "Grandma, you'll be so proud of us."

With tears in her eyes, Hazel said, "I've always been proud of you. You accepted me, and you will always be part of my family."

Back in Marin County, Hazel and David were in Hazel's home. "Hazel, I don't know what to do about the chateau. Ed and I loved it, but now with Ed gone, I have such sad memories. I don't ever want to go back there."

"Don't do anything rash. If you're thinking of selling it, the chateau is much too valuable to just dump on the market."

Dropping down onto a sofa, her eyes low, Hazel whimpered. Softly she said, "Will you stay with me until I get adjusted to a new life?"

"What do you think?"

In Omaha, Julia and Beth were unpacking from their European trip. Looking around, Beth commented, "This house is sure small compared to the places you've lived in."

"When David bought it from Mom and gave it to me, I was very grateful to get it. It's a roof over my head, free and clear."

"Except for upkeep and taxes."

Julia smiled. "Mom assured me she'd help support me until my life gets on track."

"Speaking about getting on track, when will you talk to your mother about our idea?"

Julia decided to call Ashley. "Hi, Ash, it's Mom." "What's up, Mom?"

"Can I come out and stay for a few days? I need to talk to Mom about a business idea."

"Sure, Mom, anytime. But what's this about business?"

"It's just an idea Beth and I came up with while on the tour. I'll drive up and surprise Mom."

At Hazel's house in Marin County, David and Hazel were just getting out of bed. Hazel rang for the butler.

On the speaker, the butler asked, "Yes, Mrs. Rolf?" "Coffee on the terrace, please. We'll be right down."

Stretching his arms as he sat on the edge of the bed, David asked, "Shower first?"

Hazel said, "Look outside, it's a beautiful day. Let's get into the pool."

Poolside, the butler served their coffee. Hazel said to him, "We don't need you for the rest of the morning. You can go ahead and run the household errands." The man nodded politely.

When they finished their coffee, David said, "I'll go grab my swimsuit."

With a twinkle in her eyes Hazel said, "Don't bother. Remember the great fun we had going bare-ass?"

David grinned and reached for her.

Julia drove up the driveway to Hazel's house. Nobody answered the door, so she let herself in and began searching for her mother. Eventually she wandered out to the terrace. At the sight of David and Hazel frolicking naked, her eyes bugged out and she slipped back out of sight.

She watched, spellbound, as they climbed out of the pool, moved to a lounge bed, and began sexual foreplay. When Hazel's head dropped to his crotch, Julia had to suppress a gasp. Her eyes remained glued to them, and she could not turn away as David returned the favor. As they lay immersed in lazy content and languorous after the sex, Julia slipped away.

David, his arm around her, said, "Hazel, you're a gal wonder. Or should I say, wonder girl."

Laughing, Hazel said, "I was flipping through the stations on my car radio. On a country station, they were playing a song, and the words hit home. It went something like, 'I'm not as good as I once was, but I'm as good once as I ever was.' Orally speaking, I'll always have my mouth."

David grinned. "With or without teeth." Then he added, "I hear there's nothing like it."

Hazel playfully slapped his arm.

Later, the butler returned. He said, "I see you had a guest. That's nice. We don't have many guests."

Cocking her head, Hazel said, "You must be mistaken."

"No, ma'am, I met a woman in a car. I thought she might have come from here." Hazel simply shrugged.

Later that afternoon, Hazel got a call from Ashley. She asked her grandmother, "What did you say to Mom?"

"I beg your pardon, Ash. What do you mean?"

"Mom went over to your place to talk to you. She came back crying and won't tell me what's wrong!"

"She hasn't been here." Then she paused. "Wait a minute, the butler said he met a woman in the driveway and thought I had company. Ask Julia if she has been here."

A moment later, Ashley came back on the line. "Yeah, Grandma, she said she had been there."

"Ask her if she saw David and me in the pool." A moment later, Ashley said, "She said yes." "Did she see everything?"

After another pause, Ashley said, "Yes, she did. I guess that's what got her so bent out of shape."

"Tell her I'm going to drive into the city and talk to her."

At the apartment, Hazel was just arriving to find Julia sobbing and shaking. Ashley looked confused. Hazel said, "Julia, do you want to start or should I?"

"I drove over to your house to talk to you about a business venture. No one answered the door. I went in and started looking for you. From the terrace, I saw you and David, and…"

Hazel interrupted. "I'm so sorry you had to find out about David and me."

Julia, her voice quivering, said, "Mom, please understand, I'm not mad or angry. You're adults, free to do as you please. After watching you and David, I became very mad and angry at myself. Mom, you did everything that I was unable to do with David. I am angry that I cheated him out of a happy married life. I cheated him out of having children. He stayed with me, and I used him to provide the shelter and lifestyle to live my own agenda. It's one thing to know about something, but when it is put graphically before your eyes, it's something else." Hazel demurred sadly.

Ashley joined in. "Grandma, David does have a son, who was created through love."

Hazel looked at them, thinking, then said, "If you had divorced David as soon as you understood your sexuality, I was prepared to divorce your father and live with David. When you rejected him, I willingly took your place in his bed."

Julia was again wide-eyed. "You would have divorced Dad? Why?"

"Well, in the summer, all our vacations were for fishing or visiting his relatives. In the winter, it was bowling. I begged and begged him to go to other places. He refused. I, like you, Julia, stayed for the shelter and support. He had lost all interest in sex. I had needs."

Julia asked, "When did it start between you and David?"

Hazel thought a moment. "When Ashley was five. The weekend you went to San Francisco with your lesbian friends. Through the years, all the times I said to you, "Would you ask David to call me to help with some problem?' was our secret code for a sexual encounter."

Ashley again piped in. "Mom, David is a great lover. A lot of women would be happy to have him. Except you. You threw him out with the garbage."

"I didn't look at it that way, Ash, but I can't really deny it. I guess I have nobody to blame but myself about David looking for satisfaction elsewhere."

Julia frowned and dropped her head into her hands. Then looking up, she murmured, "The more I hear, the more saddened I am for stealing his life. I can't change what I've done to him."

Hazel looked at her daughter and said, "Please don't judge him either. I will continue to have sex with him as long as my body cooperates."

Julia, turning to Ashley, said, "What about you?" Ashley was quick to answer. "I control my own life." Her mother said, "I take that as a yes."

Hazel lapsed practical now. "Now that we have everything out in the open, let's have some wine out on the balcony."

Out on the balcony, all three were momentarily swept up in the grandeur of the view.

Ashley said, "I fell in love with the city when I first saw it from the balcony. I can never thank David enough. Now I'm living here."

Hazel, lapsing thoughtful, said, "David found me the perfect man for my second life here in this apartment."

Ashley made eye contact with her, and the two exchanged a veiled smirk.

But Julia caught it. "Okay, you two. I get the point. David was very important to both of you in your San Francisco indoctrination."

Hazel smiled and said, "Now that we're through discussing the bedroom activities, what did you want to talk to me about?"

Julia cheered up. "The chateau. Beth and I would like to start an international travel agency, using the chateau as our headquarters and a hotel."

Hazel did a double take. "Where did that idea come from?"

Julia said, "When Beth and I were on the gay and lesbian European tour, we were met by reporters at every stop. We had some very high-profile people on the tour who had to drop out for fear of losing their jobs if their employers found out. Some couples took separate rooms because hotel clerks would sell room information to reporters. Some gay men and lesbian women acted as married couples. After arriving at their rooms, they would switch to their partners."

Her hand to her throat, Hazel said, "I had no idea."

Julia said, "You must have heard that spies and counterintelligence extracted a lot of classified information from gay men by threatening to make their sexuality public. So the higher the profile, the more the need for discretion. Actually, that goes for lesbians too. There are lots of lesbians in powerful positions in the government and in business these days."

Hazel was pensive. "Let me think about it overnight. Come up to the house tomorrow afternoon."

Julia said, "Okay if Beth comes along? She can be here by tonight."
"Okay," said Hazel, "she needs to be here if she's going to be involved."

A grinning Julia, now high on her idea, said, "Tomorrow afternoon it is. I sure wouldn't want to interrupt your morning swim."

Hazel wasn't listening but was gazing out over the City by the Bay.

CHAPTER TWENTY-THREE

After Julia had left, Hazel asked the butler, "Where is David?"
"I believe he's in the carriage house, tinkering with one of Ed's old cars."

In the carriage house, Hazel found David under the hood of an old right-hand- drive Morgan. She called, "David, it's me."

"I missed you." He reached out with greasy hands for her but saw her recoil. She said, "Let's wait till you clean up."

"Okay, I'll do a quick cleanup, and we can finish in the pool."

"Hmm. Speaking of the pool, Julia came by. She saw us. Everything. So for now, a swim, yes, sex, no."

"No sex?"

"Remember the song?"

He laughed. "Yeah, I do. 'I'm not as good as I once was, but I'm as good once as I ever was.'"

She said, "That's the way I feel right now. My body needs to rest a couple of days. I'm sure I can satisfy you other ways. I need some feedback from you as soon as you can tear yourself away."

Hazel retired to her study, and eventually, David came in. "I'd sure like to get that old Morgan running."

She turned to him. "David, sit down," she said as the butler rolled a cocktail cart into the room. She said, "We'll fix our own," and the butler moved off.

Turning back to David, she said, "Okay, down to business. Julia and her partner, Beth, want to turn the chateau into an international headquarters for a gay and lesbian tourist agency."

David thought it over until Hazel asked, "Your thoughts?"

"If you keep the chateau, will the emotional attachment adversely affect your health?"

Wide-eyed, Hazel said, "I don't really know. I hadn't thought about that aspect. I certainly wouldn't go there by myself. And I wouldn't want to go there with Julia and any of her friends."

"It must be very expensive to maintain. Can you afford it?"

Hazel, again looking thoughtful, said, "Let's face it, I only have a few short years to live. Yes, I can well afford to keep it. After that, it will be your problem."

"My problem?"

"Yes, darling. I've made you executor of my estate. Believe me, with all the holdings Ed left to me, you'll have a lot more than just the chateau to worry about. On second thought, let's resolve the chateau situation right now. I'll give you the chateau right now and cover all expenses until I die."

It was his turn to be pensive. "Talk about an executor 's compensation!" With a sigh, he said. "All my worries have just been resolved."

"That's it, then. I'm going to resign from the company effective immediately. Why don't you and I spend a few days at the chateau? We'd get an idea of the cost of turning it into a commercial property or even if the law will allow it."

Hazel immediately got on her phone, and David went to use his iPhone.

Talking to Julia, Hazel said, "Julia, I'll go along with your concept. David and I will go to Switzerland to check zoning laws and fees and make sure the chateau is in good condition. Anything else we should know before we leave?"

Julia said, "We'd also like a few rooms for guests for short stays." David phoned Jennifer. "I'm ready to get back to the office."

Jennifer said, "The plane will be at SFO at noon to pick up some Unidraulics people for a strategy session. I'll alert the pilot you'll be coming back with them." Turning to Hazel, David said, "I'm going to run out to Unidraulics and see Tom.

At Tom's office, Grace escorted David in.

They didn't shake hands, but David got right to the point. "Just want to touch bases before I head back to Omaha. Has anything changed between you and Ashley?"

Gazing at David, Tom said, "As much as I love Ashley, I just can't trust her to not continue bedding you. It's best if she and I go our separate ways."

Sighing, David said, "Well, I sure can't change what's happened."

Tapping his fingers on his desk, Tom replied, "Maybe after you're out of the picture, I may reconsider."

Back at his own office, David took a seat and started going through the stacks of mail. Picking up an envelope, he recognized the handwriting. Images of Pam came to mind.

> My beloved, David,
>
> My life has changed dramatically. I never knew how much I loved New Zealand and my heritage until I moved back from England. I've met a wonderful man of the same heritage. We will be married soon. David, the memories of our time together will always be precious.

Tears filled his eyes, and he folded the letter and dropped it into the shredder.

Days later, David was afforded a magnanimous farewell from the company, and he left with lots of tears, hugs, and best wishes.

In Zurich, David and Hazel sat across the desk from the court clerk for the particular canton. The clerk was looking over their proposal. He turned to them, smiling. "The government of Switzerland is very much in favor of new business. It'll cost about eight thousand Euros to get everything finalized."

David asked, "If we want to add additional private guest rooms, how is that handled?"

The clerk swiveled in his chair and said, "When the plans are submitted, we will approve them. The permit costs will be per unit."

"So as of now, the cost of starting up this venture will be eight thousand Euros, right?"

The clerk nodded and rose from his chair. "Switzerland does not judge people's lifestyles. We welcome your new business."

Later on, David and Hazel met with the building inspector at the chateau. After a thorough inspection, he said, "The buildings are in good condition. No major infrastructure problems. Overall, I'd say you should be trouble-free for several years. Now if you bring in heavy equipment, that could cause problems."

CHAPTER TWENTY-FOUR

David and Hazel were relaxing in front of the fireplace in the late afternoon. Hazel sighed. "These last few days have really tired me out. I'm going to lie down."

David saw to it that she was comfortable and left her to rest. Later he returned. "Do you feel like getting up for dinner?"

Hazel's voice was weak. "I think I'll just have something light in bed."

"Okay, darling, I'll have the staff rustle up something, and I'll eat here with you in the room."

David, without her noticing, watched Hazel as she tried to eat, but she soon lamented, "I have no appetite. I'd rather just go to sleep for now."

When she reached for him in the morning, he was already up and getting dressed.

"I don't feel like getting up today."

"No need for you to get up. I'll get you some fruit and juice to have here in bed."

"I don't know, David. I don't think I can keep it down."

Later, he checked on her and asked, "Feeling better?" The response was a weak "No, not really."

"Okay, that does it," he said. "I'm calling the doctor."

After leaving the local hospital, David was grim. The doctor had just given him some bad news on Hazel's condition. Although there were many good medical facilities in Switzerland, Hazel wanted to go home, so David arranged for a charter. He arranged for a Swiss nurse to accompany them. Sick at heart, David again looked at a slip of paper the doctor had handed him. It had one word on it: cancer.

Back in San Francisco, after a long and harrowing flight, the plane landed with a chirp of rubber and a roar of reversing engines. Hazel was taken by ambulance directly to the best hospital in San Francisco.

David was in conference with the chief oncologist on staff. He took David by the arm and, in an aside, said, "Why did you folks wait so long? Her cancer is now in an advanced stage."

David swept his hand through his hair. "She hadn't been feeling bad at all. This came on very suddenly. I got her medical attention as soon as I could. What do we do now?"

The doctor, his eyes low, said, "I'm afraid there's nothing much we can do except make her comfortable. I will refer her case to hospice immediately."

David found a place to be alone. He sat and wept copiously, his heart broken. During the second day of her hospice care, Hazel motioned for David to come close. In a weak voice, she whispered, "David, I don't want to be here. I want to go home."

David arranged for hospice care at home, and soon Hazel was home, being tended around the clock.

Late one afternoon, the nurse pushed a frail, weak Hazel in a wheelchair onto the porch to enjoy the afternoon sunshine. Hazel, pale and thin, sat wrapped in a blanket. David and the nurse, as to not bother Hazel, went to the other end of the porch and silently gazed at the vast view. Neither noticed as Hazel's hand fell to the side of the wheelchair and she slumped over. The nurse, checking her watch, remarked, "Time for meds, Hazel." She turned, saw Hazel, and screamed.

David hung his head, and the nurse sadly called her superiors and made arrangements for the coroner.

Before the nurse left, David handed her a check. She looked at it and gasped. "Sir, this is for more than three months' pay. I've only been here less than two weeks."

"Don't worry about it. One more thing: you can have this house for a one-month vacation, and I will pay the expenses while you and your family are here."

Back in his study a couple of weeks after Hazel's funeral, David was going though the estate papers when the phone rang.

"David, it's Julia. Now that the grieving has subsided, can we talk about the proposed use of the chateau?"

"Okay, Julia. As you know, I'm the executor of your mom's estate. She agreed to your project and left instructions for me to finance all aspects of the project until the day your—whatever you call it—actually starts to do business. Your mother was also very concerned that women are now giving partners HIV and other STDs."

This made Julia angry. "How could you be so cruel, saying a thing like that! I don't sleep around, changing partners. That's why I withheld sex from you, to assure Beth she wouldn't be exposed. She was sure you were sleeping around."

"So Beth was sexually blackmailing you. Funny thing, after I discovered your tit-sucking, pussy-eating lifestyle, I never had sex with you again for the same reason."

Lowering her eyes, Julia murmured, "We can't change what happened. I will always be sorry for what I did to you. How do we proceed with Beth and my plans?"

"We will need a face-to-face for the planning. You may be surprised with some of the things I have in mind."

In the San Francisco condo, David, Julia, and Beth were sitting around a table in the office. Ashley was lounging close by.

David cleared his throat to get everyone's attention. "As documented in Hazel's will, I own the chateau. You have a green light to proceed with your plans. Hazel has instructed me to finance all aspects of your project until you actually open the door for business. The financing includes you living at the chateau starting right now. I will retain the carriage house for my own personal use."

Julia and Beth exploded with joy, jumping up and hugging.

David, smiling, said, "Have you thought of a name for the business?"

"Yes," said Julia. "Rainbow Tours. We plan to put together escorted tour packages. We'll have the group meet at predetermined locations, and either Beth or I will be the tour guide."

"Sounds good, but I think you're limiting your income possibilities." Julia and Beth exchange puzzled looks. "How?" asked Julia.

David steepled his fingers and, with his chin on the peak, said, "Expand the business. Remodel the chateau so you have as many luxury suites as possible, as well as a conference room. There is also room to build twelve bungalows. How does a second name of Rainbow Retreats sound?"

The women's faces were beaming. Their reaction was pure excitement.

"Let's see—now you have tours, the hotel aspect, possibly a time-share, and conferences."

Julia and Beth gasped, overwhelmed.

Beth exclaimed, "It's all so grand. I don't have a clue how to manage that."

Julia gazed at David. "I don't either, but I know who does. David, could we put our differences aside and create a business the way you see it?"

Smiling, he said, "Your mother would like that. Of course I'll do that. You two head for Switzerland. I'll be along shortly."

As they were leaving, Julia said, "I'll give you power of attorney to sell Mom's house. Beth, let's get back to Omaha and get our passports and pack a few things."

At the Marin County home, David was in the garage, tinkering with the old right-hand Morgan, when the phone rang.

It was Ashley. "How about your son and I drive up Friday for the weekend? It may be a long time before I'm alone with you again."

As David was listening to her, an image of Hazel came into his mind. I'm not as good as I once was, but I'm as good once as I ever was. "Yeah, Ash, I'm up for it one more time."

He could almost see her grin through the phone line. "I'm sure I can get it up!" "Was there ever any doubt?"

It was a lovely day in the Swiss countryside, and at the chateau, over the next several months, the three were busy creating a business, Julia and Beth directing the creation of the luxury suites.

Beth was obsessive about things, and today she was arguing with the plumber. "I don't care what you have to do. Each bathroom must have a bidet. The bidet and toilet each must have their own private enclosure with a door!"

The plumber shook his head and called for the carpenter. The man came in and surveyed the space, figuring and measuring. He said to Beth, "I hope you have lots of money."

"Don't worry about that. Does your estimate figure a bidets-and-toilets configuration for all the twelve bungalows?"

"No, but it won't cost that much per unit as we still have time for a change order."

Beth murmured to herself, "I'd better inform David."

Julia arrived, back from her trip to the government offices. "Success," she said. "All business legal stuff is taken care of. Just need to get the construction completed and let the world know what we're about."

Beth clapped her hands in glee. "Great! Let's have a couple of our friends in advertising and marketing design our website and advertisement."

Julia said, "Good idea! They'll be able to get fast action in the gay and lesbian community."

The day the work was complete, the entrepreneurial duo walked around the premises, admiring what they had created. Julia said, "Beth, let's meet with David and let him know how thankful we are for his help."

The women, each carrying a bottle of champagne, surprised David at the carriage house. Seeing the champagne, he said, "So we're going to have a drink to your success?"

"No, to your success! This wouldn't have ever happened without your guidance."

"Well, there's one last thing I'm going to do for you. I'm paying to bring in the twelve top gay and lesbian activists for a conference so you can showcase your business."

Sometime later, the conference commenced. Julia and Beth took to the podium and explained the goals of the Rainbow Tour and Retreat.

Julia addressed the group. "I'd like to introduce the person most responsible in making all this come about: David Marsh. Some of you may or may not know, but David and I were once married. David is a straight-shooter, so you can forget any ideas you gay guys might have about a possible hookup." A ribald laugh ran through the room. "The conference is completely funded by David as a gift to Beth and me, wishing us success in our future endeavors."

Applause filled the room.

Julia said, "Wish me luck, Beth. I'm off to the Greek islands for our first tour."

Three nights later, Beth was in her suite drinking, soft mood music in the background. Caressing herself, she became aroused. Half-drunk, she got to her feet, pulled on a bathrobe, grabbed a bottle of wine, and left the room, heading for the carriage house.

David was relaxing in his recliner. Beth opened the door and staggered in, the bottle dangling from her hand.

David, looking puzzled, said, "Hi, Beth."

She didn't say a word but climbed on the recliner, pulled back her robe, exposing her naked body, and straddled his face. She murmured, "I've been wanting to rub your face in it for a long time. This time, it's for the right reason."

David obliged and did his best. After a while, she staggered a bit and sauntered out of the room, and the encounter was never mentioned again.

In the office the next day, Julia exclaimed, "What a success!"

Beth said, "I've already posted the feedback on our webpage. We've received a year and a half of bookings for the twelve Discreet Retreat bungalows. Just those bookings alone cover our operating expenses. We also have bookings for two women's and one gay men's conferences."

Julia said, "We may have to hire some tour guides. I know we'll have plenty of well-qualified applicants. I don't know if we'll be able to solve the problem with reporters dogging our tours."

Just then, David entered. "It looks like you two have everything under control. Any reason I can't return to San Francisco?"

Both women smiled. Beth said, "If we get into trouble, we can teleconference." Julia added, "Thanks to you, everything's working like a well-oiled machine." On his departure, both women walked him to the limo. They looked longingly at the elegant vehicle as it pulled away.

Back in his Marin County home, David was in the office, at his desk, the three framed pictures of Hazel, Julia, and Ashley smiling at him.

When the phone rang, it was Ashley. "Hi Ash, what's up?"

"Okay if I bring your son up to spend a week with you for some dad-and-son bonding?"

"Sure, I'd love that. We'll have a great time."

"Oh, by the way, Tom has decided that you are no longer a threat, and we want to go away for a few days and renew our vows."

David was smiling when he hung up. He sat staring at the picture. He picked up Hazel's picture and brushed his hand across it. An image of him and Hazel at the piano bar, Christopher Plummer singing, and the two of them making love on the beach brought tears to his eyes.

He next picked up Julia's picture. As he brushed his hand across it, images of Julia storming out of the club, shouting "You son of a bitch!" flooded his mind. As he set the picture down, tears continued to roll.

With Ashley's picture in hand, he brushed his hand across it, with the image in his mind of him and Ash making love in the Russian hotel room. The tears were flowing freely now as he set her picture down.

David folded his arms on the desk, rested his head on his arms, and wept uncontrollably.

It was midday at the Marin County home, and David and his young son were sitting on the porch swing, slowly swinging. Suddenly, a loud engine's roar filled the air.

They looked toward the garage. David said, "Well, it looks like the mechanic finally got the old Morgan running."

The boy leaped off the swing with glee. "Dad, how can you drive that thing with the steering wheel on the wrong side?"

"Well, son, I grew up on a farm. One of the first tractors I learned to drive was a right-hand-drive Farmall C. How about us taking the Morgan for a drive and seeing if we can find an ice cream store?"

The boy's face lit up, and he jumped off the porch.

Soon they were tooling down the road, two happy, carefree men with not a care in the world.

Printed in the United States
by Baker & Taylor Publisher Services